GIFTS IN
GOOD TASTE

GIFTS IN GOOD TASTE

Helen Hecht &
Linda LaBate Mushlin

ATHENEUM   NEW YORK

1983

Library of Congress Cataloging in Publication Data

Hecht, Helen.
    Gifts in good taste.

    Includes index.
    1. Cookery. 2. Gifts. I. Mushlin, Linda LaBate,
joint author. II. Title.
TX652.H4 1979   641.8   79-51354
ISBN 0-689-70655-3

FOR TONY AND AL,
With Love

Acknowledgments

We wish to thank our mothers, Helen D'Alessandro and Margaret Labate, for their continuing help and advice, and our forbearing children, Evan Hecht and Amy and Kate Mushlin, who tasted everything and always gave a frank opinion.

For their generous help with this book, we are also grateful to Patricia Estabrook, Patricia Ford, Carol Franklin, Elizabeth Holahan, Ida Mushlin, Sara Niemetz, Jill Stallworthy, and Molly Stern.

Contents

INTRODUCTION 3

GIFT PACKAGING 7

NOTES ON INGREDIENTS 11

QUICK BREADS ✕ 14

Apple Oatmeal Bread, Apricot Honey Bread, Blueberry Tea Cake, Christmas Tea Cake, Irish Soda Bread, Lime Tea Bread, Orange Tea Cake, Pumpkin Cider Bread, Vermont Whole Wheat Bread, Zucchini Bread

YEAST BREADS ✕ 25

Cheese Bread, Cottage Rye Bread, Country Wheat Bread, Dill Bread, Hunter's Bread, Mediterranean Herb Bread, Moroccan Bread, Pub Loaf, Sour Cream Chive Bread

CAKES 〉✖ 40

Chestnut Torte, Chocolate Chantilly Cake, Chocolate Valentine, Mother's Day Cake, Mrs. Beeton's Almond Cake, Old-fashioned Birthday Cake, Seed Cake, Tony's Birthday Cake, Twelfth Cake, Aunt Mamie's Fruit Cake, Light Fruit Cake, Mrs. Isabella Beeton's Unrivalled Plum Pudding, Hard Sauce, Spiced Fruit Cake, White Christmas Cake, Dark Christmas Cake

COOKIES AND SMALL CAKES 〉✖ 71

Chocolate Almond Thins, Chocolate-coated Tiles, Chocolate Ginger Tassies, Chocolate Wedding Cakes, Cinnamon Bows, Dream Bars, Fortune Cookies, Gertrud Blue's Brownies, Kifli, Lime Tea Cakes, Linzer Cakes, Miss Elizabeth Holahan's Fine Tea Wafers, Mocha Meringues, Nut Wafers, Orange Flower Cakes, Orange Wedding Cakes, Petits Fours, Surprise Cakes, Rolled Cookies, Apricot-filled Cookies, Chocolate Leaves

SWEET TARTS AND PIES 〉✖ 98

Flaky Pie Crust, Rich Tart Crust, Sour Cream Tart Crust, Apple Almond Tart, Chocolate Fudge Pie, Chocolate Pecan Pie, Green Grape Tart, Kentucky Sweet Potato Pie, Kiwi Strawberry Tart, Lime Tart, Nectarine (or Apricot) Custard Tart, Orange (or Banana) Chocolate Tart, Pear Chocolate Tart, Pear Cranberry (or Pear Mincemeat) Tart, Plum-Walnut Cream Tart, Strawberry Almond Tart

CONFECTIONS 〉✖ 123

Candied Grapefruit or Orange Peel, Chocolate Disks, Chocolate Easter Eggs, Chocolate (or Mocha) Fudge, Chocolate Mint Wafers, Choco-

late Truffles, Cocoa-dusted (or Chocolate-coated) Marzipan, Glazed Spiced Nuts, Pastel Mint (or Cocoa Mint) Patties, Rose Pecans, Sugarplums, Sugared Pecans, Butterscotch Sauce, Chocolate Sauce, Maple Walnut Sauce, Orange Walnut Sauce

PRESERVES 🕱 143

Rose Petal Jelly, Sage Tracklement, Sweet Violet Jelly, True Mint Jelly, Chestnuts in Brandy Syrup, Brandied Peaches, Minted Pears, Blueberry Jam, Pear Ginger Jam, Spiced Peach Jam, Strawberry Preserves, Apricot Conserve, Beet Conserve, Cranberry Orange Conserve, Pear Mincemeat, Plum Conserve, Apple Mint Chutney, Cranberry Pear Chutney, Mango Papaya Chutney, Quince Chutney, Seckel Pear Chutney

CONDIMENTS 🕱 169

Herbed Red Wine Vinegar, Basil Vinegar, Herbed White Wine Vinegar, Lemon Mint Vinegar, Sage Vinegar, Caper Sauce, Herb and Caper Mayonnaise, Othello Sauce, Pesto, Parsley Pesto, Provençal Sauce, Tomato Chutney, Lemon Dill Butter, Green Peppercorn Butter, Mustard Shallot Butter, Caper Butter

SAVORIES 🕱 182

Caponata, Chopped Chicken Livers, Chopped Chicken Livers and Mushrooms, Marinated Mushrooms, Roasted Peppers, Shrimp Butter, Smoked Salmon Spread, Smoked Trout Spread, Stilton Butter, Tarama Spread, Spiced Almonds, Spiced (or Salted) Nuts, Cheddar (or Swiss) Thins, Cheese Bits, Herb Parmesan Biscuits, Sesame Oat (or Cheddar Sesame) Crackers

PÂTÉS   🙟   197

Pâté Pastry, Aspic for Pâtés, Chicken Liver Pâté en Croûte, Duck Pâté en Croûte, Mock Game Pâté, Pâté de Campagne, Spinach Artichoke Pâté, Summer Terrine

SAVORY TARTS AND PIES   🙟   212

Pastry Crust for Savory Tarts and Pies, Artichoke Shrimp Quiche, Asparagus Quiche, Crabmeat Quiche, Leek Stilton Quiche, Mediterranean Tart, Mushroom Tart, Sea Quiche, Smoked Salmon Quiche, Spinach Roquefort Quiche, Spinach Tomato Pie, Summer Pie, Tarte à l'Oignon, Torta Rustica

POTPOURRI   🙟   229

Baker's Clay Cherry Pie, Baker's Clay Bread Basket, Mulled Cider Mix, Orange Pomander, Old Rose Potpourri, Summer Meadow Potpourri, Pine Forest Potpourri, Almond Coffee, Mocha Coffee, Orange or Lemon Coffee, Orange Spice Tea, Lemon Mint Tea, Spiced Tea, Rose Tea

GIFTS IN
GOOD TASTE

INTRODUCTION

A GIFT from your kitchen is always a welcome and appropriate gesture of friendship: it is a token of your inventive skill and imagination, and it can be infinitely adapted to suit individual tastes and preferences. Moreover, it should be as much fun to make such gifts as to give them. If you enjoy cooking, sharing what you have made with your friends will enhance that pleasure.

The idea for this book evolved because we had been in the habit of regularly sharing some innovation from our kitchens with one another, and we observed more and more of our friends giving gifts of food they had made themselves. We felt a need for a collection of special recipes designed for giving on a variety of occasions. And since we both spend more time in the kitchen than we can rationally account for, this book seemed a logical and welcome enterprise.

Dreaming up new ideas was, on the whole, easier than achieving a completely satisfactory result. We soon became eager volunteers for every school and community baked goods sale as outlets for our enthusiastic overproduction. The bakery booth at our last school fair profited handsomely from several versions of Lime Tea Bread, Fortune Cookies, and Chocolate Tiles. Our freezers are presently overburdened with more recent experiments, and it requires strategic planning simply to open and close the freezer door. As we write this, we are impatiently awaiting the next fund-raising event.

Having learned from our experiments, we have made every effort to be precise and clear in our directions. Many of the foods in this book can be made quickly and easily; others are more elaborate. But you should have no trouble in following any of the recipes included here, barring accidents of nature. One of us observed her own mother meticulously follow our recipe for a peach tart. It was baked to perfection, amber peaches encased in a nicely browned crust. As she lifted it from the oven, she accidentally dropped it on the floor. Regarding it momentarily, she shrugged her shoulders and, scooping it into a bowl, remarked, "Peach cobbler."

We have limited our selection to foods which can be transported with ease. When in doubt, we tested, providing the occasion for many family picnics. On summer afternoons we could often be found dining in some remote and wooded area on such fare as Pâté en Croûte, Asparagus Quiche, Caponata, and Nectarine Custard Tart. Other dishes were carried across a field, over a split-rail fence, and through some hedges—the shortest route between our houses.

Many of the foods in this book can be made months in advance and stored on the pantry shelf or in the freezer, so that you may always have a supply of small gifts on hand when the need arises. It is, in fact, entirely possible to have many of your Christmas gifts ready by September, and your holiday repertoire might include selections less conventional than fruit cake and cookies. Homemade chutney, for example, is a splendid accompaniment to holiday roasts, whether lamb, beef, or fowl. A selection of homemade preserves might contain a chutney, Cranberry Orange Conserve, Rose Petal Jelly, and Spiced Peach Jam, all stuffed in a grocer's wood-slatted mushroom basket. You could have in reserve an assortment of herb vinegars, jars of mincemeat, candied citrus peel, sachets and potpourri, spiced teas and coffees: the possibilities are endless.

If you want to impress your friends with a traditional English holiday sweet, we suggest you try "An Unrivalled Plum Pudding," a recipe adapted from *The Englishwoman's Cookery Book,* by the well-known Victorian authority on home and cuisine, Mrs. Isabella Beeton. Or you could give a Twelfth Cake with a bean and a pea hidden inside, in observance of an ancient British custom.

You need not, however, confine gourmet gifts to the winter holidays. One of us vividly recalls a recent birthday spent in the kitchen preparing her own cake, as well as the evening's dinner. A chocolate layer cake from a friend would have been a welcome birthday present. A Torta Rustica might sound like an unlikely gift to some, but think of the joy, perhaps even relief, it could offer your host or hostess for a summer weekend. Or you might choose to arrive bearing an exquisite glazed orange tart, its ceramic tart pan an accompanying gift, or a rich, savory Pâté de Campagne, aromatic as a summer afternoon in Provence. If you suspect that the weekend menus have been planned in advance, consider bringing something which can be enjoyed at leisure after you have left, such as a selection of breads for the freezer. Friends just pulling in from a tiring trip would certainly appreciate a fragrant onion tart from a neighbor, and any host would welcome a small basket of glazed nuts to serve with coffee. What better way to introduce yourself to new neighbors than to supply their breakfast for the morning after moving, when they probably have not yet located the carton with kitchen equipment. A thermos of coffee, a loaf of homemade bread, and a jar of jam would be a thoughtful welcome. And, to honor no particular occasion, we suggest you give a favorite chocolate lover an immoderate quantity of sumptuous Chocolate Truffles.

Next time your friends return from a vacation, or from the hospital, or have birthdays or babies, or invite you to dinner, or move to a new house, or are simply called fondly to mind, think of what you can make for them.

GIFT PACKAGING

T H E best way to wrap a gift of food is most often the simplest: the wrapping should not obscure or compete with the appeal of the food itself, but should display it in an attractive way. The wrapping need not be elaborate or expensive, and, with very little effort, it can have a personal and imaginative touch which makes your gift special. Our only admonition is not to forget the label. If your friends know what they are eating, they are more likely to enjoy it. If the gift is a sauce or an unusual jelly, it is also helpful to suggest with what foods it should be served. Here is a list of suggested wrappings or containers to give you some ideas:

1. Baskets are the most versatile of food containers. They can be found in almost any size and shape you require, whether to contain a few cookies, or a bulky selection of baked goods and preserves, and many are inexpensive. A wood-slatted mushroom basket, which costs little or nothing, is the perfect size to contain a loaf of bread, a tea cake, or a pâté baked in a loaf pan. Small

wood-slatted berry baskets can be painted in bright colors. Place a square of calico fabric inside for lining, and fill with candies, cookies, or sachets. You might even bake the basket as well as its contents! In the chapter on Potpourri, you will find directions for making one out of baker's clay. This would make a charming gift container for any homemade delicacy, and it can be used afterward as a bread basket.

2. Save your scraps of fabric. One of the prettiest ways to wrap anything in a glass jar (jams, jellies, candies, strips of candied citrus peel, sauces, etc.) is to cover the lid with a round (or square) of printed cotton fabric. While the gift is decoratively "wrapped," the content of the jar, attractive in itself, is still visible. Calico, gingham, or any small print will do. Use pinking shears if you have them, and cut the material 2 to 2½ inches larger in diameter than the top of the jar. Secure to the lid on the underside of the fabric with a bit of Scotch tape. Fasten around the collar of the lid with a rubber band, covered, if you like, with a narrow ribbon. You can do the same with a small paper-lace doily.

If you sew, you might make little sacks or Christmas stockings out of cotton or felt to hold nuts and confections.

3. A length of ribbon is often the best solution to packaging a gift. A loaf of homemade bread looks most appetizing covered with clear plastic wrap and tied with pretty ribbon. Baskets of food and even a burlap sack will look more festive when tied and bowed. Ribbon is now widely available in small flowered prints, plaids, and stripes. Or, you can make your own ties out of cotton fabric by cutting inch-wide strips with pinking shears, following the lengthwise grain of the material.

4. Always save straight-sided, wide-mouth jars, plain plastic containers, and tin cans with clear plastic lids, such as shortening or coffee cans. These might hold sauces, cocktail spreads and but-

ters, nuts, candies, etc. They can be decorated in a number of ways. Cut a rectangle, as wide as the height of the can and as long as the circumference, out of wrapping paper, wallpaper, felt, or heavy fabric and glue it around the sides of the container. Using felt and gold braid, you might decorate a can for a child to look like a drum. If you use solid-colored plastic containers, you need only tape a rosette bow to the lid to create a gift package.

5. Sturdy cardboard boxes make good containers for candies, cookies, and crackers. If it is a plain box, you need only cover the lid. Cut decorative paper large enough to fold around to the inside of the lid. Crease the edges and glue the paper to the sides of the lid and the inside edges. If you are filling the box with candies, separate the layers with lace doilies or gold foil paper. Cushion fragile items with crumpled tissue paper.

6. If you enjoy antiquing, you will often find suitable gift containers at bargain prices in antique stores, thrift shops, and at garage sales. Keep a lookout for crockery mixing bowls, cookie jars, cake or pie dishes, oval platters to hold a tea bread, candy dishes, planters, canisters, etc.

7. You can purchase very handsome and inexpensive glass bowls and cocktail tumblers at discount houseware stores, usually those selling Japanese imports. These make attractive vessels for cocktail spreads, butters, nuts, candies, and cookies. Clay flowerpots, lined with foil or plastic wrap, can be used in the same way.

8. Wrap a loaf of bread or a tea cake in a brightly patterned dish towel. Or make sacks out of pretty napkins or towels to hold any small gifts.

9. For occasions when you may want to give an expensive gift, there are a number of appropriate containers to couple with the particular food you have made. You might select a set of kitchen canisters for a bride, each filled with a different gift, such as a tea

blend, coffee blend, "wedding cake" cookies, etc. Give homemade candies in a little silver Revere bowl, a loaf of homemade bread on a wooden cutting board. Fill a picnic hamper with a loaf of bread, a pâté, caponata, and cookies or cake. A ginger jar is the perfect container for potpourri; a jam pot might accompany a homemade preserve; a wine decanter may hold an herb vinegar. A canvas tote bag is practical as a sack for loaves of bread, fruit cakes, or any large items. A tart or pie can be given in its baking dish—aluminum, glass, or ceramic—or, unmolded, on a china serving dish. Fill a pretty teapot or coffeepot with one of the tea or coffee blends. China teacups and demitasse cups make special containers for any small items, such as glazed or salted nuts. Small gifts can also be cached in a wide variety of beautiful boxes, such as Indian brass boxes, Mexican tin or glass hinged boxes, fabric-covered or lacquered boxes, china or silver boxes. Buy a flower bowl, jardiniere, salad bowl, vegetable dish, or even an ice bucket to hold a plum pudding, fruit cake, Twelfth Cake, or a batch of small cakes or cookies.

Look around and you will be surprised at how many ideas occur to you. A beautifully wrapped gift only takes a little imagination.

NOTES ON INGREDIENTS

ALMOND PASTE Do not substitute for almond paste what is labeled "marzipan," as it is too sweet.

BRANDY Most of our recipes specify using brandy instead of cognac. If you use a good-flavored brandy, this seems a justifiable economy.

BUTTER Unsalted butter is almost always specified in our recipes and it is especially important in baking. Read the label carefully when buying it, as butters are often labeled "sweet" when they are lightly salted rather than unsalted.

CHEESE If you are buying a prepackaged Cheddar cheese, select "extra sharp," as those labeled "sharp" are usually too mild to use effectively in recipes.

Always be cautious in selecting Swiss cheese, and if it is not prepackaged, ask to taste it first. Many have very little flavor.

Always use freshly grated Parmesan cheese. You can grate your own and keep it indefinitely in the freezer, and it need not be defrosted before using. The prepackaged grated Parmesan is either flavorless or too salty. If buying Parmesan from a wheel, it is advisable to taste it first, as some varieties are very salty.

CHOCOLATE   Use only pure chocolate, not "chocolate flavored." Chocolate chips contain added ingredients and cannot be used interchangeably with pure chocolate.

CITRUS RIND   Grate as much rind as needed or accumulate larger amounts by peeling the fruit with a vegetable peeler, drying it, and then grating it in a blender or food processor. Keep grated rind in the freezer. Never use commercially bottled rind.

EGGS   All recipes are based on U.S.D.A.-graded large eggs.

FLOUR   Unless otherwise specified, use "unbleached, all-purpose" flour in all recipes requiring flour. It is higher in nutritional value than bleached flour and the two can be used interchangeably. However, unbleached hard wheat flour, available in health food stores, is more desirable for baking yeast breads.

HERBS   Use fresh herbs when possible. Salad spinners make it easy to wash and dry large quantities of fresh herbs.

LEMON OR LIME JUICE   Always use fresh lemon or lime juice; the bottled juice with added preservatives has an artificial flavor.

MAPLE SYRUP   Use pure maple syrup, not what is sold as "pancake syrup."

NUTS   To store for long periods of time, keep nuts in the freezer; it is not necessary to defrost them before using. To toast, place on a baking sheet and bake in a preheated oven at 350° for 5 minutes, or until lightly browned.

ORANGE FLOWER WATER   Orange flower water can be bought in specialty food stores, particularly those which sell Middle Eastern foods.

ROSE HIPS, HIBISCUS, AND PURE ROSE FLAVOR   Rose hips, hibiscus, and pure rose flavor can be bought in the spice departments of many supermarkets or in specialty food stores.

ROSE WATER   Rose water can be bought in specialty food stores and, frequently, in drugstores.

STEEL-CUT OATS   Several of our recipes call for "steel-cut oats." These are available in health food stores and are often sold in supermarkets as "Irish oatmeal." The hard, nutty kernels retain a distinct texture after baking, and you should not substitute rolled or instant oats.

SYNTHETIC FLAVORINGS   Wherever possible, we have tried to use pure, natural ingredients.

QUICK BREADS

BREADS which use baking powder or baking soda as their leavening agent are not what we usually think of as breads. Crumbly in texture and usually sweetened, they are more often "tea cakes" which have been baked in a loaf pan. They are easy to make and require no particular instruction except the caution to fold the flour into the batter gently and not to overmix, or the bread will not have a light texture.

Measure flour by pouring or spooning it into a dry-measure cup and leveling off with a knife.

Cooking times are always approximate, as ovens vary. Always test with a skewer before the total baking time has elapsed. When done, the loaf will have shrunk a bit from the sides of the pan.

Quick breads freeze successfully. To defrost, unwrap the loaf and set it on a wire rack so that the moisture can evaporate.

For gift giving, consider using miniature loaf pans and giving each recipient a selection of several small loaves. Remember to adjust the baking time accordingly. Start checking with a skewer after 20 minutes.

You may successfully double any of the quick bread recipes.

APPLE OATMEAL BREAD

This is a crisp, wholesome loaf, and makes an appealing fall gift. Because of its coarse texture, it has a tendency to crumble and should therefore be cut in thick slices with a serrated knife.

2 cups rolled oats
1½ cups flour
½ cup firm-packed light brown sugar
3½ teaspoons baking powder
1½ teaspoons cinnamon
½ teaspoon salt
¾ cup vegetable oil
2 eggs, beaten
1 cup apple cider
2 cups fine-chopped peeled apples (3 medium)
⅔ cup fine-chopped walnuts or pecans

Preheat oven to 350°.

Measure the oats, flour, brown sugar, baking powder, cinnamon, and salt into a large bowl and mix well. In another bowl, beat together the vegetable oil and eggs. Stir in the cider, apples, and nuts, and fold into the dry ingredients. Turn into a greased 9-by-5-inch loaf pan and smooth the top with a spatula. Bake for about 1 hour, or until a skewer inserted in the center comes out clean. Cool in the pan on a wire rack.

YIELD: ONE LOAF

✂ APRICOT HONEY BREAD

The honey and apricots combine to form a dark, moist bread that keeps for several days. It is sweet enough to serve for afternoon tea or substantial enough to complement a light soup at lunch or supper.

3/4 cup hot water	Grated rind of 1 medium
1 1/2 cups dried apricots	orange
2 1/4 cups flour	1 cup light honey
2 teaspoons baking	1 egg
powder	1/2 cup coarse-chopped
3/4 teaspoon baking soda	walnuts

Preheat oven to 325°.

Pour the hot water over the apricots and let stand at least 30 minutes. Butter and flour a 10½-by-5½-inch loaf pan.

Sift together the flour, baking powder, and baking soda. Add the orange rind. Drain the apricots well, reserving the water. Add the honey to the apricot water and stir until mixed. Stir in the egg. Add the honey mixture to the flour mixture and stir with a fork until well combined. Chop the apricots coarse and add. Stir in the walnuts. Pour into the prepared pan and bake 55 to 65 minutes, or until lightly browned and the sides pull away from the pan. Cool in the pan on a wire rack.

YIELD: ONE LOAF

❧ BLUEBERRY TEA CAKE

This is a particularly nice gift when accompanied by a jar of homemade Blueberry Jam (page 154).

4 tablespoons unsalted butter, softened	1½ cups flour
¾ cup sugar	1 cup blueberries, washed and dried, with stems removed
2 eggs, separated	
2 teaspoons grated lemon rind	1 teaspoon baking powder
½ teaspoon vanilla extract	½ teaspoon baking soda
	¼ teaspoon salt
	½ cup sour cream

FOR THE TOPPING
Approximately 1 teaspoon sugar

Preheat oven to 350°.

Cream the butter; add the sugar gradually and beat until light and fluffy. Add the egg yolks, lemon rind, and vanilla, and beat well. Mix 2 tablespoons of the flour with the blueberries. (Coating the berries with flour prevents them from sinking to the bottom of the cake.) Sift the rest of the flour with the baking powder, baking soda, and salt. Add the flour to the batter alternately with the sour cream, beginning and ending with the flour. Beat the egg whites until stiff. Stir one quarter of the beaten whites into the batter. Fold in the remainder. Carefully fold in the blueberries and turn into a greased 8½-by-4½-inch loaf pan. Sprinkle the surface with about 1 teaspoon granulated sugar. Bake for about 50 minutes, or until a skewer inserted in the center of the loaf comes out clean. Cool in the pan on a wire rack.

YIELD: ONE LOAF

✘ CHRISTMAS TEA CAKE

This orange-flavored quick bread, speckled with tart cranberries, is an appropriate gift anytime cranberries are in season. We specify using temple oranges since they are a cross between oranges and tangerines, and therefore a compromise between a rind that is easy to grate and tangerine-flavored juice. You may certainly use tangerines instead, if you can find them with skins taut enough to be grated.

4 tablespoons unsalted butter, softened
¾ cup sugar
2 eggs
Grated rind of 1 temple orange
2 cups flour
1½ cups coarse-chopped cranberries

¾ teaspoon baking powder
½ teaspoon baking soda
¼ teaspoon salt
⅔ cup temple orange juice

Preheat oven to 350°.

Cream the butter with the sugar until fluffy. Beat in the eggs, one at a time, with an electric mixer until the mixture is very light. Add the grated orange rind. Mix 2 tablespoons of the flour with the chopped cranberries. Sift the remaining flour with the baking powder, baking soda, and salt. Add the flour mixture to the batter alternately with the orange juice, beginning and ending with the flour. Fold in the cranberries until just blended; do not overmix. Pour into a well-greased 9-by-5-inch loaf pan and bake for about 1 hour, or until a skewer inserted in the center of the loaf comes out clean. Cool in the pan on a wire rack.

YIELD: ONE LOAF

⚭ IRISH SODA BREAD

This is a versatile quick bread, equally good as a picnic or supper loaf, or for breakfast, spread with sweet butter and jam. While it has many of the attributes of a yeast bread, it can be made very quickly and easily.

4 cups flour	*3 tablespoons unsalted*
⅔ cup steel-cut or Irish	*butter, chilled and cut*
oats	*into small pieces*
2½ teaspoons salt	*1½ to 1¾ cups*
1 teaspoon baking soda	*buttermilk*

Preheat oven to 400°.

Measure the flour, oats, salt, and baking soda into a large mixing bowl and stir to blend thoroughly. Cut in the butter with a pastry blender or rub it into the flour quickly with the tips of your fingers. Stir in 1½ cups buttermilk gradually, mixing with your hands as the dough becomes stiff. Add a little more buttermilk if the dough is too dry; it should feel firm, but slightly moist. Do not overwork it. Pat it into a round loaf, about 8 inches in diameter, and cut an X across the surface of the loaf to a depth of about ½ inch. Place it on a lightly greased baking sheet and bake for about 50 minutes, or until the loaf sounds hollow when tapped and a skewer inserted in the center comes out clean. Cool on a wire rack.

YIELD: ONE ROUND LOAF

✖ LIME TEA BREAD

The tart lime flavoring makes this an unusual tea bread. You may substitute lemon, but we urge you to try it first with lime.

6 *tablespoons unsalted*	*1½ cups flour*
butter, softened	*1½ teaspoons baking*
1 cup sugar	*powder*
Grated rind of 2 large	*¼ teaspoon salt*
limes (1½	*⅔ cup milk*
tablespoons)	*⅔ cup coarse-chopped*
2 eggs	*walnuts*

Preheat oven to 350°.

Cream the butter and beat in the sugar with an electric mixer until light. Add the grated lime rind and the eggs and beat well. Sift the flour with the baking powder and salt and add it to the batter alternately with the milk, beginning and ending with flour. Fold in the chopped nuts and turn into a greased 8½-by-4½-inch loaf pan. Bake for 45 to 55 minutes, or until a skewer inserted in the center of the loaf comes out clean. Cool in the pan on a wire rack.

YIELD: ONE LOAF

❧ ORANGE TEA CAKE

This is a sweet tea cake with a glazed orange top. Beating the egg whites separately gives it a light and springy texture.

¼ pound unsalted butter,
  softened
¾ cup sugar
2 eggs, separated
Grated rind of 1 large or
  2 small oranges

1½ cups flour
1½ teaspoons baking
  powder
¼ teaspoon baking soda
¼ teaspoon salt
½ cup orange juice

FOR THE GLAZE
¼ cup orange juice
¼ cup sugar

Preheat oven to 350°.

Cream the butter. Add the sugar gradually, beating with an electric mixer until light. Beat in the egg yolks, one at a time, and the grated orange rind. Sift the flour with the baking powder, baking soda, and salt, and add it to the batter alternately with the orange juice, beginning and ending with flour. Beat the egg whites until stiff and fold them carefully into the batter. Pour into a greased 8½-by-4½-inch loaf pan and bake for 50 to 60 minutes, or until a skewer inserted in the center of the cake comes out clean.

While the cake is baking, make the glaze. Combine the orange juice and sugar in a small saucepan. Simmer gently for 5 to 10 minutes, stirring occasionally, until a light syrup forms. Spoon the hot syrup over the cake as soon as it is removed from the oven. Cool in the pan on a wire rack.

YIELD: ONE LOAF

🎀 *PUMPKIN CIDER BREAD*

A sweetened tea bread, for giving in the fall.

2 eggs
¼ cup vegetable oil
¾ cup light brown sugar
¼ cup apple cider concentrate, defrosted but not diluted, or 1 cup apple cider boiled down to equal ¼ cup
1 cup cooked, mashed pumpkin, fresh or canned
Grated rind of 1 orange

2 cups flour
2 teaspoons baking powder
¼ teaspoon baking soda
½ teaspoon salt
¼ teaspoon mace
¼ teaspoon cinnamon
⅛ teaspoon ground cloves
½ cup coarse-chopped walnuts

Preheat oven to 350°.

Beat the eggs with the oil. Add the sugar, cider, mashed pumpkin, and orange rind and beat well. Sift the flour with the baking powder, baking soda, salt, and spices and fold into the pumpkin mixture. Stir in the nuts. Bake in a well-greased 8½-by-4½-inch loaf pan for about 1 hour, or until a skewer inserted in the center of the loaf comes out clean. Cool in the pan on a wire rack.

YIELD: ONE LOAF

✕ VERMONT WHOLE WHEAT BREAD

This is a hearty New England–style quick bread in which the maple syrup, while very subtle in flavor, adds a fine and moist texture.

¾ cup vegetable oil	½ cup white flour
¾ cup pure maple syrup	1½ teaspoons baking
2 eggs	powder
½ cup milk	½ teaspoon baking soda
1½ cups whole wheat	¾ teaspoon cinnamon
flour	½ teaspoon salt
¼ cup cracked wheat	⅔ cup coarse-chopped
¼ cup steel-cut oats	pecans

Preheat oven to 350°.

Mix together the vegetable oil, maple syrup, eggs, and milk. In another mixing bowl, combine the whole wheat flour, cracked wheat, and oats. Sift together the white flour, baking powder, baking soda, cinnamon, and salt and combine this with the whole wheat flour mixture. Pour in the liquid mixture and the chopped pecans and mix all together gently until just blended. Turn into a well-greased 9-by-5-inch loaf pan and bake for about 65 minutes, or until a skewer inserted in the center comes out clean. Cool in the pan on a wire rack.

YIELD: ONE LOAF

❌ ZUCCHINI BREAD

A moist tea loaf with a mild spice flavor. It is good spread with cream cheese.

3 ounces cream cheese, softened	*Grated rind of 1 lemon*
3 tablespoons vegetable oil	*2¼ cups flour*
1 cup sugar	*1 teaspoon baking soda*
2 eggs	*¾ teaspoon cinnamon*
1 cup shredded or coarse-grated unpeeled zucchini	*½ teaspoon nutmeg*
	¼ teaspoon salt
	½ cup dark seedless raisins

Preheat oven to 350°.

Beat together the softened cream cheese, oil, and sugar. Add the eggs, one at a time, and continue beating until the mixture is light. Stir in the zucchini and lemon rind. Sift the flour with the baking soda, cinnamon, nutmeg, and salt and fold into the batter gently, taking care not to overmix. Finally, fold in the raisins, mixing only until blended. Turn the batter into a well-greased 8½-by-4½-inch loaf pan and bake for approximately 1 hour and 15 minutes, or until a skewer inserted in the center comes out clean. Cool in the pan on a wire rack.

YIELD: ONE LOAF

YEAST BREADS

I F you have never baked a loaf of yeast bread, do not be intimidated by the prospect. There is no mystery to bread baking; and while experience, as in every cooking technique, is of value, there is no reason why you can't produce a respectable loaf at the outset. The recipes we have developed are not difficult and do not require the level of expertise that a loaf of real French bread, for example, might demand. The following are basic techniques and procedures you should know before you begin:

1. *Proofing yeast:*
Granulated "instant blend" active dry yeast is the easiest to use. Most recipes call for one packet. To activate the yeast, it should be dissolved in ¼ cup warm water from the tap. "Warm" is not scalding; nor is it the tepid temperature you would use for a baby's bath. It should register between 110° and 115° on a thermometer. Too high a temperature will kill the yeast; in too

low a temperature it will not be activated. To test or "proof" it, a little sugar is stirred into the yeast water. After a few minutes, the mixture should swell and bubble up at the surface. If it fails to do so, throw it out and start again, adjusting the water temperature. Better to waste a packet of yeast than a loaf of bread.

2. *Mixing the dough:*

Except in recipes where otherwise specified, the dough should not be either dry or sticky; it should feel firm and slightly damp after mixing. Add the flour gradually until you feel you have the proper consistency. As the batter becomes stiff, mix with your hands. If you flour, oil, or dampen your hands with water, the dough will not stick as much.

3. *Kneading:*

If you cover the dough after mixing and let it rest for 10 minutes, it will be less sticky and easier to work with. When ready to knead, place it on a floured surface. Flatten it with the heel of your hand, pushing it away from you as you do so. Turn it a quarter turn, and fold it over on top of itself from back to front. Continue pushing, turning, and folding for 5 to 7 minutes, or until the dough feels smooth and elastic. As you are kneading, dust the work surface with a little additional flour as often as necessary to prevent the dough from sticking.

4. *Rising:*

Place the dough in a greased mixing bowl large enough to allow for expansion. Turn it over to grease the top surface. Cover the bowl with plastic wrap and put it in a warm, draft-free place to rise. We find an unheated oven, with the oven light left on, a convenient place to set the dough to rise. If it is a cold day, fill a large pan with hot water and place it in the oven on a rack below the dough. During the first rising, the dough should more than double in volume and become very light and porous. Blisters will appear on the surface. This could take 1 to 2 hours, or more, depending on the temperature. Times given for rising in the individual recipes are only guidelines. After the first rising, the dough is literally "punched down" with your fist to deflate it. You should then roll it out on a floured board, and roll it up tightly to form a loaf, pinching the seams to seal. Next, it is set to rise again in a greased loaf pan until it has just doubled. This usually does not take as long as the first rising. If you are using the correct size loaf pan, the center of the loaf should dome slightly above the top edge of the pan. If the finished loaf is to have a sheen, it is then brushed with a glaze, and it is ready for baking.

5. *Baking:*

Place the loaves in the center of a preheated oven, well spaced if you are baking more than one. When the bread is done, it will sound hollow when tapped and a skewer inserted in the loaf will test clean. Remove the loaf from the baking pan. It should feel firm; if it tends to collapse a bit, put it back into the pan and continue baking. If you want to brown the bottom and sides of the loaf, remove it from the pan and set it directly on the oven rack for a few minutes. When done, always turn it out of the pan immediately to cool on a wire rack.

All our bread recipes may be doubled, but if you are a novice, it will be easier to work with a smaller amount of dough, following the proportions for one loaf. It is best to bake no more than two loaves at a time in one oven; crowding is likely to produce a lopsided or misshapen loaf. All yeast breads may be frozen if well wrapped. To defrost, unwrap and set on a wire rack.

❧ CHEESE BREAD

This cheese bread has a pronounced Cheddar flavor and is moist and light in texture. It is good as a sandwich bread, or toasted and buttered, or warmed in the oven.

1 package active dry yeast
1 cup warm water
1 teaspoon sugar
3 cups flour
1 teaspoon salt

8 ounces extra sharp
Cheddar cheese, grated
coarse (2 cups,
packed)

FOR THE GLAZE AND GARNISH
1 egg white beaten with 1 tablespoon water
Sesame seeds

Dissolve the yeast in ¼ cup of the warm water; stir in the sugar and set aside to proof. Measure the flour and salt into a mixing bowl. Stir in the remaining ¾ cup water and the yeast mixture. The dough should be moist, but if it is too sticky to knead, add 1 or 2 more tablespoons flour. Let the dough rest for 10 minutes. Turn onto a floured board and knead for 6 to 8 minutes until smooth and elastic, sprinkling additional flour on the board when necessary to prevent sticking. Place the dough in a greased bowl, turn over to grease the surface, and cover the bowl with plastic wrap. Let rise for 1 to 2 hours, or until it is 2½ times its original volume. Punch down and knead in the cheese, sprinkling on a little at a time and distributing it evenly through the dough. Roll into a rectangle approximately 8 by 12 inches, and roll up from the short side so that you have a loaf 8 inches long. Pinch the seams to seal and place, seam side down, in a well-greased 8½-by-4½-inch loaf pan. Lightly oil the top of the loaf, cover with plastic wrap, and let rise for 1 hour, or until double in volume The center of the loaf should crest above the rim of the pan.

Preheat oven to 350°.

Brush the egg white glaze over the top of the loaf and sprinkle with sesame seeds. Bake for 45 to 55 minutes, or until the loaf sounds hollow when tapped and a skewer tests clean. To brown the sides and bottom, remove the loaf from the pan and set it on the oven rack for the last 5 minutes of baking. Cool out of the pan on a wire rack.

YIELD: ONE LOAF

✄ COTTAGE RYE BREAD

1 package active dry yeast	*1 tablespoon lemon juice*
¼ cup warm water	*1 egg*
1 teaspoon sugar	*2 teaspoons caraway*
2 tablespoons unsalted	*seeds*
butter, softened	*¾ teaspoon salt*
1 cup creamed cottage	*¼ teaspoon baking soda*
cheese, at room	*¾ cup rye flour*
temperature	*2 to 2¼ cups white flour*

FOR THE GLAZE

1 egg white beaten with 1 tablespoon water

Dissolve the yeast in the warm water. Stir in the sugar and allow to proof. Combine the softened butter, cottage cheese, lemon juice, egg, caraway seeds, salt, and baking soda, beating to blend well. Mix in the rye flour. Stir in the yeast mixture. Gradually beat in 1 3/4 cups of the white flour to make a slightly moist dough. Sprinkle a board with flour, and knead for 6 or 7 minutes, adding up to 1/2 cup additional white flour, as necessary, to prevent sticking. Place in a greased bowl, turning the dough over to grease the surface. Cover the bowl with plastic wrap and set in a warm place to rise for about 1 1/2 hours, or until doubled. (Rye flour rises more slowly than white.) Punch down, pat the dough into a rectangle about 8 by 12 inches, roll up from the short side, and pinch the seams to seal. Place in a well-greased 8 1/2-by-4 1/2-inch loaf pan, seam side down, oil the surface of the loaf lightly, cover the pan with plastic wrap, and let rise until doubled. The center of the loaf should rise just above the rim of the pan.

Preheat oven to 350°.

Brush with the egg white glaze. Bake for 40 to 45 minutes, or until the loaf sounds hollow when tapped and a skewer comes out clean. Turn out of the pan and cool on a wire rack.

YIELD: ONE LOAF

✖ COUNTRY WHEAT BREAD

This is a hearty whole grain bread. It is best toasted and spread with butter and jam or honey. Unlike most whole wheat breads, this one is light in texture.

1 package active dry yeast
1 cup warm water
¼ teaspoon sugar
1 egg
*2 tablespoons vegetable
  oil*
2 tablespoons light honey
1 tablespoon molasses
½ cup steel-cut oats

¼ cup cracked wheat
*¼ cup coarse-chopped
  sunflower seeds*
1 teaspoon salt
½ cup white flour
*2¼ cups whole wheat
  flour, preferably stone
  ground*

Dissolve the yeast in ¼ cup of the warm water; stir in the sugar and allow to proof. Meanwhile, beat the egg lightly and combine it in a large mixing bowl with the remaining ¾ cup water, the vegetable oil, honey, and molasses. Stir in the oats, cracked wheat, chopped sunflower seeds, salt, and white flour. Add the yeast mixture and mix well. Gradually add up to 2¼ cups whole wheat flour, mixing thoroughly with your hands. The dough should be quite moist. Do not add more flour. Place it in a greased bowl, turning the dough over to grease the top. Cover with plastic wrap and allow to rise in a warm place for about 1½ hours, or until doubled in bulk. (Whole wheat flour takes longer to rise than white.) Punch down the dough and roll it out on a floured board into a rectangle approximately 8 by 12 inches. Roll it up from the short side to form a loaf 8 inches long. Pinch the seams to seal and place, seam side down, in a well-greased 9-by-5-inch loaf pan. Lightly oil the surface of the loaf; cover it with plastic wrap, and let it rise in a warm place for about 1 hour, or until doubled in bulk. The center of the loaf should just crest over the top of the loaf pan.

Preheat oven to 350°.

Bake for 45 minutes, or until the loaf sounds hollow when tapped and a skewer inserted in the center comes out clean. Turn out onto a wire rack to cool.

YIELD: ONE LOAF

⚜ *DILL BREAD*

This is a popular light bread that is easy to make and does not require kneading. It should be toasted and spread with sweet butter.

1 package active dry yeast	*½ teaspoon salt*
¼ cup warm water	*¼ teaspoon baking soda*
2 tablespoons sugar	*1 cup creamed cottage*
1 tablespoon unsalted	*cheese, at room*
butter, softened	*temperature*
2 tablespoons minced	*1 egg*
yellow onion	*2½ cups flour*
2 teaspoons dried dill	
weed	

Dissolve the yeast in the warm water and stir in 1 tablespoon of the sugar. Allow to proof. In a large bowl, mix the remaining sugar, the softened butter, minced onion, dill weed, salt, baking soda, cottage cheese, and egg. Stir in the yeast mixture and add the flour slowly, mixing well with your hands. (The dough will be sticky and it will be easier to manage if you rub your hands with vegetable oil or rinse with tap water before handling it.) Place it in a greased bowl, lightly oil the surface of the dough, cover with plastic wrap, and let rise in a warm place for 1 to 1½ hours, or until more than doubled in volume. Punch down and place on a well-floured board. Roll or pat into a rectangle approximately 12 by 8 inches. Roll up from the short side, pinch seams to seal, and place, seam side down, in a very well-greased 9-by-5-inch loaf pan. Lightly oil the surface of the loaf, cover with plastic wrap, and let rise for about 30 minutes, or until just doubled.

Preheat oven to 350°.

Bake for about 1 hour. If the bread browns too quickly, cover loosely with aluminum foil during the latter part of baking. When done, the bread should sound hollow when tapped and a skewer inserted in the center should come out clean. Remove from the baking pan and cool on a wire rack.

YIELD: ONE LOAF

✘ HUNTER'S BREAD

This is a highly aromatic bread which goes well with stews and roast fowl. We call it Hunter's Bread because it is strongly flavored with rosemary, an herb commonly used in Italy for the preparation of game dishes.

1 package active dry yeast	¾ cup dry white wine
¼ cup warm water	2½ teaspoons dried
1 teaspoon sugar	rosemary
1 egg	1 teaspoon salt
2 tablespoons olive oil	3 to 3¼ cups flour

FOR THE GLAZE
   1 egg white beaten with 1 tablespoon water

Dissolve the yeast in the warm water and stir in the sugar. Allow to proof. Meanwhile, beat the egg lightly and stir in the olive oil, wine, rosemary, and salt. Mix in 2 cups of the flour, then stir in the yeast mixture. Gradually add enough of the remaining flour, mixing with your hands, to make a soft but workable dough. Knead it on a lightly floured board for about 5 to 8 minutes, dusting with additional flour only if necessary to prevent sticking. The dough should feel smooth and elastic. Place it in a greased bowl, turning it over to grease the top. Cover the bowl with plastic wrap and let the dough rise in a warm place for about 1 hour, or until more than doubled in bulk. Punch it down and roll it out on a floured board into a rectangle approximately 8 by 12 inches. Roll it up from the short end to form a loaf 8 inches long. Pinch the seams to seal and place, seam side down, in a well-greased 8½-by-4½-inch loaf pan. Lightly oil the surface of the loaf, cover with plastic wrap, and let it rise in a warm place until doubled in bulk. The center of the loaf should just crest above the top of the pan.

Preheat oven to 350°.

Brush the loaf with the egg white glaze and bake it for 45 to 50 minutes. When done, the loaf should sound hollow when tapped and a skewer inserted in the center should come out clean. Turn out onto a rack to cool.

YIELD: ONE LOAF

✖ MEDITERRANEAN HERB BREAD

This aromatic bread goes well with summer salads, as well as with heartier soups and stews.

1 package active dry yeast
¼ cup warm water
1 teaspoon sugar
¼ cup minced raw onion
2 teaspoons tarragon
2 teaspoons chervil
½ teaspoon thyme
1 teaspoon salt

1 egg
2 tablespoons olive oil
¾ cup milk, scalded and
returned to room
temperature
⅓ cup fresh-grated
Parmesan cheese
3¼ cups flour

FOR THE GLAZE
1 egg white beaten with 1 tablespoon water

Dissolve the yeast in the warm water; stir in the sugar and allow to proof. In a large mixing bowl, combine all remaining ingredients except the flour. Beat in the yeast mixture. Add the flour gradually, mixing well with your hands. The dough will be moist. Allow it to rest for 10 minutes. Turn onto a floured board and knead for 6 to 8 minutes, sprinkling with additional flour to prevent sticking, until the dough feels smooth and elastic. Place in a greased bowl, turning over to grease the surface. Cover with plastic wrap and set in a warm place to rise for 1 hour, or until more than doubled in volume. Punch the dough down and roll it out on a floured board into a rectangle approximately 8 by 12 inches. Roll it up from the short side to make a loaf 8 inches long. Pinch the seams to seal and place, seam side down, in a well-greased 8½-by-4½-inch loaf pan. Lightly oil the surface of the loaf; cover with plastic wrap and let rise for 30 to 45 minutes, or until doubled. The center of the loaf should crest above the rim of the pan.

Preheat oven to 350°.

Brush the top of the loaf with egg white glaze. Bake for 45

to 50 minutes, or until the loaf sounds hollow when tapped and a skewer inserted in the center comes out clean. Turn out of the pan and cool on a wire rack.

YIELD: ONE LOAF

✖ MOROCCAN BREAD

A coarse-textured round bread, nice for picnickers.

1 package active dry yeast   *½ cup cracked wheat*
1 cup warm water   *2 tablespoons sesame*
1 teaspoon sugar   *seeds*
2 cups white flour   *1 teaspoon salt*
½ cup whole wheat flour   *Cornmeal*

Dissolve the yeast in ¼ cup of the warm water. Stir in the sugar and allow to proof. Combine the flours, cracked wheat, sesame seeds, and salt and stir in the yeast mixture, plus the remaining warm water. Knead the dough for 6 to 8 minutes until it feels elastic. With your hands, pat it into a flat, round loaf, approximately 1 inch high and 6 inches in diameter. Place it on a cookie sheet dusted with cornmeal; cover with a clean dish towel and let rise in a warm place for 2 hours, or until doubled.

Preheat oven to 400°.

Bake the loaf for 15 minutes. Lower the heat to 325° and bake 20 minutes longer, or until the loaf sounds hollow when tapped and a skewer comes out clean. Cool on a wire rack.

YIELD: ONE ROUND LOAF

✕ PUB LOAF

The Muenster cheese in this bread, while not pronounced in flavor, gives it a chewy and porous texture, rather like that of a French bread. Reheated in the oven in aluminum foil, it is a good dinner bread.

1 package active dry yeast	*2 tablespoons mayonnaise*
1 cup warm water	*1 teaspoon dried thyme or*
1 teaspoon sugar	*sage (leaf, not rubbed)*
4 ounces Muenster cheese,	*1 teaspoon salt*
grated coarse (1 cup,	*2¾ cups flour*
packed)	

FOR THE GLAZE
1 egg white beaten with 1 tablespoon water

Dissolve the yeast in ¼ cup of the warm water and stir in the sugar. Allow to proof. Meanwhile, combine the Muenster cheese, mayonnaise, thyme or sage, salt, and ¾ cup water. Stir in 1 cup of the flour, then add the yeast mixture. Mix in the remaining flour gradually, using your hands as the dough becomes stiff. Turn it onto a lightly floured board and knead for about 6 minutes, or until the dough feels elastic and is no longer sticky. Dust the board with additional flour, if necessary, while kneading to prevent the dough from sticking. Place the dough in a greased mixing bowl, turn it over to grease the top, cover the bowl with plastic wrap, and let it rise in a warm place for about an hour, or until more than doubled in bulk. Punch the dough down and roll it out on a floured board into a rectangle approximately 8 by 12 inches. Pinch the seams to seal, and place, seam side down, in a well-greased and lightly floured 8½-by-4½-inch loaf pan. Lightly oil the surface of the loaf, cover it with plastic wrap, and let it rise until doubled in bulk. The center of the loaf should just crest over the top of the pan.

Preheat oven to 350°.

Paint the surface of the loaf with the egg white glaze. Bake for about 50 minutes, or until the loaf sounds hollow when tapped and a skewer inserted in the center comes out clean. Turn out onto a wire rack to cool.

YIELD: ONE LOAF

SOUR CREAM CHIVE BREAD

A moist, light bread, which is good for sandwiches or toasted and buttered.

1 package active dry yeast
¼ cup warm water
1 tablespoon sugar
1 cup sour cream, at room
   temperature
1 tablespoon butter,
   melted

1 tablespoon lemon juice
1 teaspoon salt
¼ teaspoon baking soda
3 tablespoons chopped
   fresh or freeze-dried
   chives
3 to 3¼ cups flour

FOR THE GLAZE
   1 egg white beaten with 1 tablespoon water

Dissolve the yeast in the warm water. Stir in the sugar and let proof. Mix together the sour cream, melted butter, lemon juice, salt, baking soda, and chives. Beat in 2 cups of the flour and then add the yeast mixture. Gradually mix in enough of the remaining flour to make a soft dough. Let the dough rest for 10 minutes. Turn onto a floured board and knead for 6 to 8 minutes until smooth, sprinkling the board with additional flour, if necessary, to prevent sticking. Place in a greased bowl, turn over to grease surface, cover the bowl with plastic wrap, and let rise in a warm place for 1 to 1½ hours, or until more than doubled in bulk. Punch down and pat or roll the dough on a floured board into a rectangle, 8 by 12 inches. Roll up from the short side to make a loaf 8 inches long. Pinch the seams to seal, and place, seam side down, in a well-greased 8½-by-4½-inch loaf pan. Lightly oil the top of the loaf and cover the pan with plastic wrap. Let rise 45 minutes to an hour, or until the center of the loaf has just crested over the rim of the pan.

Preheat oven to 350°.

Brush with egg white glaze and bake for 40 to 50 minutes, or until the loaf sounds hollow when tapped and a skewer inserted in the center comes out clean. Turn out of the pan and cool on a wire rack.

YIELD: ONE LOAF

CAKES

HAVE all ingredients ready, at the proper temperature, and measured before you begin the cake. For example, if the recipe calls for melting chocolate or butter, do that first so that it will have a chance to cool.

Measure dry ingredients by ladling or pouring them into the cup and leveling off with a knife or spatula. If a recipe calls for *sifted* flour, measure the flour by sifting directly into the measuring cup and leveling off. Use measuring cups intended for dry ingredients for flour and sugar and measuring cups intended for liquids for milk and water. It is difficult to obtain accurate results when you use the wrong type of cup. Check liquid ingredients at eye level to ensure accuracy.

Follow instructions exactly. Don't skimp on the time that it takes to cream butter or to beat eggs. The amount of air beaten into an ingredient is an important component of a cake. On the other hand, don't beat more than is necessary to accomplish the task. Overbeating can cause a cake to become heavy. When folding ingredients into whipped eggs, do so quickly and gently so that you don't deflate the eggs. Using a wide rubber or plastic spatula, cut down through the center of the eggs and quickly bring the eggs up and over the top. Give the bowl a quarter turn and repeat. Repeat as many times as is necessary to blend the ingredients. Be certain that the cake is mixed thoroughly. Don't leave any pockets of dry ingredients or melted butter at the bottom of the bowl. If you do, the cake will bake with a soggy bottom or may collapse. We have found that proper mixing is most easily done in a wide-bottomed bowl with gently sloping sides.

If you butter the cake pans with your fingers, you can be more certain that the butter will be evenly distributed. Spread the batter evenly in the cake pans and tap the pans gently on the counter top to remove any air bubbles. Don't try to crowd the pan. Fill a cake pan only three fourths full to allow for rising during baking.

Bake one cake layer in the center of the oven. If baking two layers, position them diagonally in the oven, making certain that the pans don't touch. It is important that the air in the oven circulates freely around each cake pan.

Do not rely solely on the baking time given in the recipe. Ovens differ, and a temperature difference of 25 degrees can reduce or increase the baking time substantially. When a cake tester or wooden skewer inserted into the center of the cake comes out dry, the cake is done. Overbaking results in a dry, choky cake; underbaking can cause a cake to collapse or to be soggy and sticky. If you are uncertain about your oven's reliability, use an oven thermometer.

Don't remove a cake from the pan right from the oven. A hot cake may crumble and fall apart. Cool it in the pan for at least

5 minutes before trying to remove it. If the directions call for cooling the cake completely before removing from the pan, loosen it gently first. That way it won't stick when you take it out. Always cool a cake on a rack so that the air can circulate freely. This prevents it from becoming soggy on the bottom.

Refrigerate all cakes made with a whipped cream filling or frosting, and in hot weather, refrigerate those made with butter cream frostings.

When transporting a cake, set toothpicks into the top of the frosting to keep plastic wrap from touching the surface.

✄ CHESTNUT TORTE

This has the texture of a moist sponge cake. The chestnut flavor is very delicate and the topping for the cake should not overpower it. We suggest serving it with slightly sweetened whipped cream, flavored with crème de cacao or cocoa. Do not substitute canned chestnut purée for the fresh chestnuts; it is too moist and produces a soggy, dense cake.

3/4 pound fresh chestnuts
5 eggs, separated
3/4 cup sugar
3 tablespoons crème de cacao, preferably white

1/2 cup plain cracker crumbs, not salty or greasy (Uneeda Biscuits or Bremner Wafers, for example)
1/8 teaspoon cream of tartar

Cut an **X** with a sharp knife into the flat side of each chestnut. Cover the chestnuts with water and boil for 15 minutes, or until they are tender. Shell and skin while warm. Purée them in a food processor or blender. You should have 1 ⅓ cups of purée, packed.

Preheat oven to 350°. Butter and lightly flour a 7- or 8-inch round cake pan.

Beat the egg yolks with an electric mixer for several minutes until lemon colored. Add the sugar gradually and continue beating until the mixture is very light and thick. Fold in the crème de cacao, puréed chestnuts, and cracker crumbs. Beat the egg whites with the cream of tartar until they are stiff. Carefully fold the beaten whites into the batter, incorporating them thoroughly, but do not deflate them. Turn into the prepared cake pan and bake for 40 to 45 minutes, or until the cake springs back when pressed lightly in the center. A skewer inserted in the center should come out clean. Cool in the pan on a wire rack.

YIELD: ONE ROUND SINGLE-LAYER CAKE

✖ CHOCOLATE CHANTILLY CAKE

This is an elaborate cake, perfect for a very special birthday. It is a layer cake, filled with whipped cream and covered with a hard chocolate icing. It can be covered and transported very easily.

FOR THE CAKE

¾ cup sifted flour
½ cup sifted unsweetened cocoa
¼ teaspoon salt
1 tablespoon instant coffee powder, preferably espresso

2 teaspoons vanilla extract
7 tablespoons unsalted butter, melted
6 eggs, at room temperature
1 cup sugar

FOR THE FILLING

2 cups heavy cream, chilled

¼ cup confectioners' sugar

1 tablespoon brandy

½ package unflavored gelatin (1½ teaspoons)

¼ cup cold water in a very small pan or a heat-resistant measuring cup

1 ounce unsweetened chocolate, shaved or grated

FOR THE ICING

⅓ cup sugar

1 tablespoon light corn syrup

3 tablespoons water

¾ cup confectioners' sugar

1 tablespoon egg white, generous

1 tablespoon unsalted butter, melted

2 ounces unsweetened chocolate, melted

1 teaspoon vanilla extract

TO MAKE THE CAKE

Preheat oven to 350°. Butter and flour two round 8- or 9-inch cake pans.

Sift together the flour, cocoa, salt, and coffee into a small bowl. Add the vanilla to the melted butter.

Combine the eggs and sugar in a large metal or ceramic bowl. Set the bowl over a pan of barely simmering water. Do not let the water boil or the eggs will cook. Stir for several minutes until the eggs are warm to the touch. Remove the bowl from the heat and beat with an electric mixer for 12 to 15 minutes, or until the mixture has tripled in volume and has the creamy consistency of very lightly whipped cream. Remove from the heat and sprinkle one half of the flour mixture over the top. Fold in very gently so that you don't deflate the eggs. Repeat with the remaining flour mixture. Pour in the melted butter, folding it in as you do so. Make sure that all ingredients are thoroughly incorporated and that no pockets remain in the bottom of the bowl.

Pour the batter into the prepared pans and bake approximately 20 to 25 minutes, or until a skewer inserted in the center comes out dry.

Cool in the pans on a wire rack for 5 minutes, then invert onto the rack by running a knife along the sides and tapping gently on the bottom of the pan with a knife.

TO MAKE THE FILLING

When the cake layers are completely cooled, whip the cream until foamy. Add the confectioners' sugar and the brandy and whip until the cream is almost set. The beaters should leave ripples in the cream; but stop beating while the cream is still too soft to hold its shape. Sprinkle the gelatin over the cold water. Set the pan or cup over very low heat and stir until the gelatin is completely dissolved, about 3 minutes. Cool, stirring, for about 2 minutes. Pour into the partially whipped cream and immediately finish whipping the cream. Stir in the shaved chocolate.

Work quickly now, since the gelatin will set. Place one cake layer on a large flat plate or board. Spread about one third of the cream on top, smoothing it as much as possible. Gently place the second layer on top of the cream. Don't press down. Spread the remaining cream on the top and sides of the entire cake, making it as smooth and symmetrical as possible. The cream on top should have a thickness of about ½ inch. Place the cake, without removing it from the board, in the refrigerator for at least 30 minutes while the cream sets.

TO MAKE THE ICING

Place the sugar, corn syrup, and water in a small saucepan. Heat, stirring, until the sugar dissolves. Cook over medium heat until the liquid is clear, about 10 to 15 minutes. Wash the sides of the pan with a pastry brush dipped in cool water.

Pour the syrup into the top of a double boiler. Add the confectioners' sugar and stir until it is dissolved. The mixture will be thick. Place the pan over, not in, simmering water and stir until smooth. Add the egg white, melted butter, melted chocolate, and vanilla, and stir with a wooden spoon or spatula for 2 to 3 minutes, or until the mixture is smooth. Keep over warm water until ready to use, but do not allow the icing to get too hot. It should be just warm enough to pour. If too hot to the touch, stir it, off the heat, for 1 to 2 minutes before using.

TO ICE THE CAKE

When the cream is set, remove the cake from the refrigerator. Gently transfer it to a cake rack which has been placed over waxed paper. Stir the icing if a crust has formed and be sure that it is smooth. Quickly pour the warm icing over the cake, holding the pan about 2 to 3 inches above the center of the cake. The icing should spread over the top and down the sides. If some areas on the sides are not covered, quickly scoop up some of the icing falling on the paper and carefully spread it on the bare spots.

Don't press on the cream. The result should be a smooth, shiny covering. Let set for a few minutes, then carefully transfer the cake to its serving or transporting dish and refrigerate until the icing is set. It can be refrigerated overnight, if necessary. The cake should be kept refrigerated, but can stand at room temperature for 2 to 3 hours without harm. Slice with a back and forth motion rather than pressing down on the cake.

YIELD: ONE ROUND DOUBLE-LAYER CAKE

✖ CHOCOLATE VALENTINE

Inside the pastel pink exterior of this valentine hides an unexpected dark and creamy chocolate cake. The frosting is a mint-flavored whipped cream, held firm by the addition of a little gelatin. It successfully covers the chocolate cake, and yet is neither too rich nor too sweet. It is stable enough to transport without any trouble.

To make the valentine, you will need a heart-shaped baking pan which has a 5- to 6-cup capacity: that is, a volume equal to that of an 8- or 9-inch round layer cake pan. Such pans are available in aluminum foil.

FOR THE CAKE

6 ounces German's sweet baking chocolate
¼ pound unsalted butter
4 eggs
¾ cup sugar

¼ cup cake flour
2 tablespoons cocoa
⅓ cup ground pecans
1 tablespoon brandy

FOR THE FROSTING

1 teaspoon unflavored gelatin	*1 cup heavy cream, chilled*
2 tablespoons cold water	*2 drops of red food coloring, optional*
2 tablespoons sugar	
½ teaspoon peppermint extract	

TO MAKE THE CAKE

Preheat oven to 350°.

Break up the chocolate and put it with the butter in the top of a double boiler over simmering water. Stir constantly until melted, remove from heat and cool to room temperature.

Using the heart-shaped pan as a pattern, cut out a piece of waxed paper to fit the bottom of the pan. Grease and flour it and set it inside the cake pan, greased side up.

Combine the eggs and sugar in a mixing bowl and set the bowl over a pan of barely simmering water. Do not let the water boil or the eggs will cook. Stir for several minutes until the eggs are warm. Remove the bowl from the heat and beat with an electric mixer for 12 to 15 minutes, or until the mixture is tripled in volume. Put the melted and cooled chocolate and butter into a large, wide-bottomed mixing bowl. Then turn the beaten eggs carefully into the same bowl. Sift the flour and the cocoa together over the eggs. Sprinkle in the ground pecans and brandy and fold everything together gently, incorporating all the chocolate into the batter, but being careful not to deflate the beaten eggs. Turn into the waxed paper-lined heart pan and bake for 30 to 40 minutes. When done, the edges of the cake will be dry and the center will be slightly moist. Be careful not to overcook it. Cool in the pan on a wire rack. The surface of the cake will crack as it cools. When cool, loosen the edges of the cake with a knife and carefully invert it onto a flat plate, cracked side down. Frost the smooth side.

TO MAKE THE FROSTING

In a small, heat-proof cup, soften the gelatin in the cold water and then dissolve it over low heat. Allow it to cool to room temperature. Meanwhile, add the sugar and the peppermint extract to the cream and beat it until it begins to thicken. Pour in the dissolved gelatin and continue beating until thick. Add food coloring if desired. Spread the whipped cream evenly over the cooled cake, covering it completely and swirling a decorative design on the surface. Do this as soon as the frosting has been made and before it has had a chance to set. Refrigerate until firm and return to room temperature before serving.

YIELD: ONE SINGLE-LAYER CAKE

MOTHER'S DAY CAKE

Mothering Day has long been observed in England and originated among the working children:

> Three centuries ago Mid-Lent Sunday, the fourth Sunday in Lent, was recognized in country places as a day when apprentices and daughters in service were set at liberty to return home for the day, and customarily they brought home with them some small token of filial affection. . . . The traditional gift on Mothering Sunday is a bunch of violets,

and the traditional fare is Simnel Cake, a rich, saffron-flavored fruit cake with almond icing. . . .*

Our Mother's Day Cake is an Americanized version, encased in almond paste and decorated with candied violets. We have omitted the saffron and use strawberries, which seem the most seasonal fruit for our own May holiday.

FOR THE CAKE
- 1 ¼ cups sifted flour
- ¼ teaspoon salt
- 2 teaspoons vanilla extract
- Grated rind of 1 medium lemon
- 6 tablespoons unsalted butter, melted
- 6 eggs, at room temperature
- ¾ cup sugar

FOR THE FILLING
- 1 cup strawberries, ripe but not soft
- 2 cups heavy cream, chilled
- ¼ cup confectioners' sugar
- 1 tablespoon sweet sherry
- ½ package unflavored gelatin (1 ½ teaspoons)
- 3 tablespoons cold water in a very small pan or heat-resistant cup

FOR THE COVERING
- ⅓ cup confectioners' sugar (to dust the table)
- 14 ounces almond paste, not marzipan
- 3 to 4 drops food coloring, optional
- Candied violets

* Iona and Peter Opie, *The Lore and Language of School Children* (London: Oxford University Press, 1959), pp. 241–243.

TO MAKE THE CAKE

Preheat oven to 350°. Butter and flour two round 9-inch cake pans.

Sift the flour with the salt into a small bowl. Stir the vanilla and the lemon rind into the melted butter.

Combine the eggs and sugar in a large metal or ceramic bowl. Set the bowl over a pan of barely simmering water. Do not let the water boil or the eggs will cook. Stir for several minutes until the eggs are warm to the touch. Remove the bowl from the heat and beat with an electric mixer for 12 to 15 minutes, or until the mixture has tripled in volume and has the consistency of very lightly whipped cream. Remove from the heat and sprinkle one half of the flour over the top. Fold in very gently so that you don't deflate the eggs. Repeat with the remaining flour. Pour in the melted butter, folding it in as you do so. Make sure that all ingredients are thoroughly incorporated and that no pockets remain in the bottom of the bowl.

Pour the batter into the prepared pans and bake about 20 to 25 minutes, or until a skewer inserted into the center of the cake comes out dry. Cool in the pan on a wire rack for 5 minutes, then invert onto the rack by running a knife along the edges and tapping gently on the bottom of the pan with a knife. Cool completely before proceeding.

TO MAKE THE FILLING

Wash and hull the strawberries. Slice each in half and place, cut side down, on paper toweling to dry.

When the strawberries are dry, whip the cream until foamy. Add the sugar and sherry and whip until the cream is almost set. The beaters should leave ripples in the cream; but stop while the cream is still too soft to hold its shape. Sprinkle the gelatin over the water. Set over low heat and stir until the gelatin is dissolved, about 3 minutes. Cool, stirring, for 2 to 3 minutes. Pour into the partially whipped cream and finish whipping the cream. Work quickly now, since the gelatin will set.

Place one layer of the cake on a large flat plate or board. Spread about one third of the cream on top, making it as smooth and level as possible. Arrange the strawberries on top of the cream in one layer. Gently place the second layer of cake on top of the berries. Don't press down. Spread the remaining cream over the top and sides of the entire cake, trying to make it as smooth and symmetrical as possible. The cream on top should have a thickness of about ½ inch. Place the cake, without moving it from the board, in the refrigerator for at least 30 minutes to set the cream. It can be refrigerated overnight. While it is chilling, prepare the covering.

TO PREPARE THE COVERING

Sprinkle the confectioners' sugar on your work surface. Soften the almond paste by kneading it with your hands, if necessary. Form it into one large ball, kneading in the food coloring, if desired. Place it on top of the sugar and roll it out with a rolling pin to a circle large enough to envelop the entire cake.

TO ASSEMBLE

When the cream has set, remove the cake from the refrigerator. Gently set the sheet of almond paste on top of the cake, being careful to center it. Wrap the almond paste around the sides, allowing it to fall into folds. Smooth the paste all over and trim any edges. Dampen a towel and brush lightly over the entire surface to remove any powdered sugar. Decorate with the candied violets. The cake must be kept refrigerated, but may stand at room temperature for several hours without harm. It is surprisingly sturdy and can be transported easily.

Note: Instead of the candied violets, the cake may be decorated with sugared fruit or other candied flowers. It can even be baked in square cake pans and "tied" with a marzipan bow.

YIELD: ONE ROUND DOUBLE-LAYER CAKE

✖ MRS. BEETON'S ALMOND CAKE

A moist cake to serve at tea or whenever you want a light dessert. Serve with confectioners' sugar dusted over the top and with slightly sweetened and brandy-flavored whipped cream on the side.

½ pound blanched almonds (scant 2 cups)
6 tablespoons unsalted butter, softened
½ cup plus 2 tablespoons sugar
6 eggs, separated

1 teaspoon almond extract
Grated rind of 1 medium lemon
6 tablespoons flour
Pinch of cream of tartar

Preheat oven to 350°. Butter and lightly flour a 7- or 8-inch round cake pan.

In a food processor or blender, grind the almonds, a little at a time, to a powder. Cream the butter and beat in the sugar gradually. Beat in the egg yolks one at a time, and continue beating until the mixture is very light. Stir in the almond extract and grated lemon rind. Fold in the flour and ground almonds. Beat the egg whites with a pinch of cream of tartar until stiff. Stir one quarter of the beaten whites into the batter. Fold in the rest of the egg whites very gently, so as not to deflate them, but thoroughly. Pour into the prepared cake pan and bake for 40 to 50 minutes. The cake is done when it springs back when pressed lightly and when a skewer inserted in the center comes out clean. Cool in the pan on a wire rack.

YIELD: ONE ROUND SINGLE-LAYER CAKE

OLD-FASHIONED BIRTHDAY CAKE

A two-layer white sponge cake frosted with chocolate butter cream.

4 eggs
2 cups sugar
1 teaspoon vanilla
    extract
2 cups sifted cake
    flour
1/4 teaspoon salt
2 teaspoons baking
    powder

3 tablespoons unsalted
    butter, melted
1 cup hot milk
1 recipe Chocolate
    Butter Cream
    (page 56)

Preheat oven to 350°. Butter and flour two 9-inch round cake pans.

Beat the eggs with the sugar and vanilla until very light. Sift together the flour, salt, and baking powder. Stir the melted butter into the hot milk. Beat one half of the flour mixture into the eggs and then beat in one half of the hot milk mixture. Beat in one half of the remaining flour mixture, then the rest of the milk. Finally, beat in the remaining flour. Pour into the prepared cake pans and bake for approximately 30 minutes, or until a wooden toothpick inserted into the center of the cake comes out clean. Cool for 5 minutes in the pan, then invert onto a rack. When completely cool, spread the top of one layer with butter cream. Top with the second layer and spread the remaining butter cream over the top and sides.

This recipe can be doubled.

YIELD: ONE ROUND DOUBLE-LAYER CAKE

✖ SEED CAKE

Dating from Elizabethan times, and perhaps earlier, it was the custom in England to have seed cakes on the Eve of All Saints, or Halloween, which marked the end of wheat seed time. Our Seed Cake is like a pound cake and is flavored with caraway seeds and brandy. It is adapted from Isabella Beeton's nineteenth-century English cookbook.

½ pound unsalted
   butter, softened
¾ cup sugar
3 eggs
2 cups sifted flour
2 teaspoons baking
   powder

½ teaspoon nutmeg
Pinch of mace
2 tablespoons caraway
   seeds
⅓ cup brandy

Preheat oven to 350°. Butter an 8½-by-4½-inch loaf pan.

Cream the butter with the sugar. Add the eggs, one at a time, and beat the mixture until light and fluffy. Resift the flour with the baking powder, nutmeg, and mace. Stir the caraway seeds into the flour mixture. Beginning and ending with the flour, add the flour and the brandy alternately to the batter. Turn into the prepared loaf pan and bake for about 1 hour, or until a skewer inserted in the center comes out clean. Cool in the pan on a wire rack.

This recipe may be doubled.

YIELD: ONE LOAF CAKE

✕ TONY'S BIRTHDAY CAKE

This is a four-layer torte filled with almond cream and chocolate butter cream and it is always made for Tony Hecht's birthday. You may, of course, make it for whomever you like and on any occasion. But we do not like to encourage substitutions, and the cake will not be authentic unless it bears the legend Happy Birthday, Tony.

FOR THE ALMOND FILLING
7 ounces almond paste, not marzipan
3 tablespoons unsalted butter, softened
2 teaspoons brandy
¼ cup heavy cream, chilled

FOR THE CHOCOLATE BUTTER CREAM
6 ounces German's sweet baking chocolate
½ cup heavy cream, chilled
2 tablespoons sugar

2 teaspoons vanilla extract
3 egg yolks
6 tablespoons unsalted butter

FOR THE CAKE

1½ cups walnuts
(¾ pound)
¼ cup flour
¾ cup sugar
7 egg whites

⅛ teaspoon cream of
tartar
1 teaspoon vanilla
extract

TO MAKE THE ALMOND FILLING

Knead the almond paste with your fingers to soften it. Then beat
it with a wooden spoon until it is smooth. Beat in the softened
butter and the brandy. Whip the cream until it is stiff and fold it
into the almond mixture. Refrigerate until firm.

TO MAKE THE CHOCOLATE BUTTER CREAM

Break up the chocolate and put it in the top of a double boiler
with the cream, sugar, and vanilla. Stir until the chocolate is
melted over hot (not boiling) water. Remove from the heat and
stir in the egg yolks, one at a time. Cook over simmering water,
stirring constantly, for 5 minutes. Remove from heat, cool for a
minute or two, and stir in the butter by small bits. Chill until it is
firm enough to spread, but not too stiff.

TO MAKE THE CAKE

Preheat oven to 300°.

Grind the walnuts coarsely or chop *very* fine by hand. Mix the
nuts with the flour and sugar. Beat the egg whites until frothy; add
the cream of tartar and continue beating until stiff. Beat in the
vanilla. Carefully fold in the nut mixture, combining well, but
do not deflate the egg whites. Spread evenly in a greased and
lightly floured 10-by-15-inch jelly roll pan. Bake for 40 minutes

until dry and very slightly colored, but not browned. Cool in the pan on a wire rack.

TO ASSEMBLE

Cut the cake into four strips, each 10 inches long and 3¾ inches wide. Divide the almond filling in half and spread over two of the layers. Spread a coating of chocolate butter cream over a third layer. Assemble the cake with an almond-frosted layer on the bottom, a chocolate-frosted layer next, then another almond layer, and the unfrosted layer on top. Spread the remaining chocolate butter cream over the top and sides of the cake. Swirl a design into the butter cream on top of the cake, if you like. Refrigerate until ready to serve.

YIELD: ONE 4-LAYER TORTE

❃ TWELFTH CAKE

The twelfth day after Christmas is the feast of the Epiphany honoring the Magi, the three kings from the East who journeyed to Bethlehem to pay tribute to the Christ Child. It has been the custom for many centuries in Great Britain and on the Continent to celebrate "La Fête des Rois" by serving a Twelfth Cake, a confection containing a hidden token, by which an honorary king and queen were chosen. In his *Observations on Popular Antiquities,* the English historian John Brand cites a sixteenth-century source on this custom:

> The materials of the cake are flour, honey, ginger, and pepper. One is made for every family. The maker thrusts in,

at random, a small coin as she is kneading it. . . . Whoever finds the piece of coin in his share is saluted by all as king, and, being placed on a seat or throne, is thrice lifted aloft with joyful acclamations.*

There were, of course, variations in the tradition: the Twelfth Cake was often a "plum," or fruit, cake, and a bean and pea, designating the king and queen, were hidden in it instead of a coin. An ancient Greek and Roman custom of drawing lots for kingdoms, practiced at this time of year, was integrated with the Christian tradition by means of this cake.

Our recipe is like a pound cake, incorporating the ingredients cited by Brand. We recommend, as somewhat less hazardous, the use of a bean and pea rather than a coin. The cake looks most festive if it is baked in a fancy ring mold and decorated with glacéed fruit and blanched almonds to resemble a jeweled crown. A written explanation of the custom should accompany this gift.

½ pound unsalted butter, softened	½ teaspoon ginger
2½ cups sugar	3 cups flour
2 tablespoons light honey	1 scant teaspoon salt
5 eggs, separated	A dried bean
Grated rind of 1 large lemon	A dried pea
1 teaspoon fresh- and fine-ground black pepper	1 cup buttermilk
	¼ teaspoon baking soda
	2 tablespoons hot water

* John Brand, with the additions of Sir Henry Ellis, *Observations on Popular Antiquities* (London: Chatto & Windus, 1913), p. 14.

FOR THE DECORATION
¼ cup light corn syrup
Whole blanched almonds
Glacéed fruit such as whole red and green cherries

Preheat oven to 325°. Butter and flour an 8- to 10-cup bundt pan
or decorative ring mold.

Cream the butter, adding the sugar gradually, and beat until
light and fluffy. Beat in the honey and the egg yolks, one at a
time. Add the lemon rind, pepper, and ginger. Measure the flour
and salt, and sift them together twice. Add the bean and pea to the
flour. Beat the egg whites until stiff and set aside. Beginning and
ending with the flour, add flour and buttermilk alternately, in
three and four parts, to the batter. Before adding the last ⅓ cup
of buttermilk, stir ¼ teaspoon baking soda dissolved in 2 tablespoons hot water into the batter. Finally, fold in the beaten egg
whites. Pour into the prepared pan and bake for 1 hour and 15
minutes to 1 hour and 25 minutes, or until a skewer inserted in
the cake comes out clean. Cool the cake in the pan on a wire rack
for 5 minutes. Then run a knife around the outside edges and
inner tube to loosen the entire cake. Cool 15 minutes longer;
turn out of the pan onto the rack and complete cooling before
decorating.

TO DECORATE

Heat the corn syrup and brush it over the surface of the cake. Stud
with fruit and almonds to resemble the jewels in a crown.
YIELD: ONE LARGE BUNDT OR TUBE CAKE

Fruit Cakes

✂ AUNT MAMIE'S FRUIT CAKE

This is a light batter fruit cake with dried rather than candied fruits.

One 15-ounce package   3 eggs
    dried mixed fruit   ¾ cup sugar
1 cup hot water   ¾ cup vegetable oil
1¾ cups flour   ½ cup broken-up
2 teaspoons baking   walnuts, lightly
    powder   toasted

Preheat oven to 350°. Butter and flour a 9-by-5-inch loaf pan or a 5-cup ring mold.

Soak the dried fruit in the hot water for at least 30 minutes. Drain and chop coarsely.

Sift together the flour and the baking powder. Beat the eggs until light. Gradually add the sugar and beat until ribbons form. Beat in the flour and the oil alternately, beginning and ending with the flour. Stir in the fruit and nuts. The batter will be stiff. Pour into the prepared pan and bake for 40 to 50 minutes, or until a skewer inserted into the center comes out dry. Cool in the pan on a wire rack.

This recipe can be doubled.

YIELD: ONE LOAF CAKE

✕ LIGHT FRUIT CAKE

This is a very good American type of fruit cake: a coffee cake batter filled with glacéed fruits and nuts. Because of the high proportion of fruit, it is best to cut it with a serrated knife.

2 cups glacéed cherries
3/4 cup coarse-chopped
  candied pineapple
1 cup coarse-chopped
  candied or dried
  apricots
1/2 cup golden raisins
1/2 cup slivered
  blanched almonds
2 1/2 cups flour
1/4 pound unsalted
  butter, softened

3/4 cup sugar
2 eggs
1 1/4 cups sour cream
2 tablespoons orange
  marmalade
Grated rind of 1 lemon
1/2 teaspoon baking
  powder
1/2 teaspoon baking
  soda
1/4 teaspoon salt
Dry sherry

FOR THE DECORATION
1/4 cup light corn syrup
Reserved cherries and pineapple

Preheat oven to 325°. Butter and flour a 7- to 8-cup ring mold.

Combine cherries, pineapple, apricots, raisins, and almonds with 1/2 cup of the flour, reserving a few of the cherries and pineapple pieces for decoration. In another bowl, cream the softened butter and beat in the sugar very gradually until the mixture is light and fluffy. Beat in the eggs, one at a time, and then add the sour cream, marmalade, and grated lemon rind. Sift the remaining 2 cups flour with the baking powder, baking soda, and salt and combine with the batter. Fold in the fruit and nut mixture. Spread

the batter evenly in the prepared ring mold and bake for 50 to
60 minutes, or until a skewer inserted in the cake comes out clean.
Loosen the edges of the cake from the mold with a knife, and cool
it in the pan on a wire rack before unmolding. When cool, sprinkle the cake, top and bottom, with a little dry sherry. Cover, let
stand for several days, and sprinkle with sherry again. If well
wrapped, this cake will keep for several weeks in a cupboard or
refrigerator.

TO DECORATE

Before giving the cake, warm the corn syrup, brush it over the
top of the cake, and decorate with the reserved cherries and pineapple.
This recipe may be doubled.
YIELD: ONE LARGE RING CAKE

❧ MRS. ISABELLA BEETON'S UNRIVALLED PLUM PUDDING

Isabella Beeton, in her nineteenth-century *Englishwoman's Cookery Book,* gives us four recipes for plum pudding, classified as follows: "Baked Plum Pudding," "Christmas Plum Pudding (very
good)," "An Excellent Plum Pudding," and "An Unrivalled Plum
Pudding." After very little deliberation, we chose the last and offer
it here with American measurements, slightly modified, and reduced by half to a quantity we thought more practical.
  Plum puddings are known for their capacity to keep, and it is
not unusual in England to make them a year in advance. They
are traditionally served with Hard Sauce, for which a recipe follows.

14 ounces currants
(approximately 2¾
cups)
¾ pound golden raisins
(approximately 2¼
cups)
½ pound dark raisins
(approximately 1½
cups)
3 ounces mixed candied
peel (approximately
⅓ cup)
⅔ cup blanched
slivered almonds,
optional

Grated rind of 2 lemons
1 tablespoon nutmeg
2 tablespoons cinnamon
2 cups sugar
1 pound fresh bread
crumbs
1 pound suet, chopped
fine
8 eggs
½ cup brandy
1 teaspoon almond
extract

Put the currants, raisins, candied peel, almonds, lemon rind, spices, sugar, bread crumbs, and suet in a large mixing bowl. In a separate bowl, beat the eggs lightly, and stir in the brandy and almond extract. Pour this into the fruit mixture and stir with a wooden spoon until well mixed.

Grease very well and flour two 2-quart or one 4-quart pudding mold. Pack in the pudding mixture very firmly. (Molds should be no more than three quarters full.) Cover the molds tightly with greased and floured lids or heavy aluminum foil. Put them on racks or in colanders inside very deep pots. Pour boiling water into the pots to come halfway up the sides of the molds. Cover the pots tightly and set on top of the stove to boil for 6½ hours. Replenish with more boiling water during cooking, as necessary. After cooking, remove the molds from the water and cool for 30 minutes. Run a knife all around the inside edges of the mold to loosen, and unmold the pudding.

TO GIVE THE PUDDING

Cover it completely in a double thickness of heavy aluminum foil, tying securely at the top. Attach instructions to reheat before serving, as follows:

Place the foil-covered pudding on a rack or in a colander in a deep kettle. Poor in boiling water to reach halfway up the sides of the pudding. Cover the kettle and keep the water simmering for 1 hour. If desired, heat ½ cup brandy, ignite with a match, and pour over pudding before serving.

This recipe may be doubled.

YIELD: ONE LARGE OR TWO SMALL PLUM PUDDINGS

✖ HARD SAUCE

An accompaniment to plum pudding. Keep it in the refrigerator and allow to soften slightly before serving. A little of this goes a long way. The quantity below should be sufficient for one 2-quart pudding.

¼ pound unsalted butter, softened
⅔ cup confectioners' sugar
Grated rind of 1 medium lemon
2 tablespoons brandy

Cream the softened butter. Add the sugar gradually and beat until light and fluffy. Mix in the lemon rind and brandy.

YIELD: ABOUT ¾ CUP HARD SAUCE

✖ SPICED FRUIT CAKE

This is a medium-dark fruit cake, with a very mildly spiced batter. It is laden with fruits and nuts and should be sliced with a serrated knife.

½ cup dark seedless
  raisins
⅓ cup brandy
2 cups flour
2 cups glacéed red
  cherries
1 cup coarse-chopped
  candied pineapple
¾ cup coarse-chopped
  dates
1 cup coarse-chopped
  pecans
½ cup coarse-chopped
  walnuts

¼ pound unsalted
  butter, softened
¾ cup dark brown
  sugar, packed
3 eggs
2 tablespoons orange
  marmalade
2 teaspoons baking
  powder
1½ teaspoons
  cinnamon
¾ teaspoon nutmeg
¼ teaspoon salt
Brandy, rum, or
  bourbon

FOR THE DECORATION
¼ cup light corn syrup
Reserved cherries and pecans

Preheat oven to 325°. Butter and flour a 7- to 8-cup ring mold.

Heat the raisins and brandy in a small saucepan and simmer for a few minutes. Remove from the heat and let stand while you prepare the cake.

Mix ½ cup of the flour with the cherries, pineapple, dates, pecans, and walnuts, reserving a few of the cherries and pecans to decorate the cake. In a large bowl, cream the softened butter. Add the sugar gradually and beat until fluffy. Beat in the eggs, one at a time. Add the marmalade. Drain the raisins, reserving the brandy. Add water to the brandy to equal ½ cup liquid. Add the raisins to the fruit and nut mixture. Sift the remaining 1½ cups of flour with the baking powder, cinnamon, nutmeg, and salt. Beginning and ending with the flour mixture, fold the flour and the brandy and water alternately into the batter. Finally, fold in the fruit and nut mixture. Spread the batter evenly in the prepared ring mold and bake for 50 to 60 minutes, or until a skewer inserted in the center comes out clean. Run a knife between the edges of the cake and the pan to loosen. Cool in the pan on a wire rack. After the cake has cooled, unmold it and sprinkle, top and bottom, with a little brandy (or, if you prefer, rum or bourbon). Cover, let stand for several days, and sprinkle with brandy again.

TO DECORATE

Before giving the cake, warm the corn syrup, brush it over the top of the cake, and decorate it with the reserved cherries and pecans. This cake will keep for several weeks in the cupboard or refrigerator.

This recipe may be doubled.

YIELD: I LARGE RING CAKE

The two fruit cakes which follow are fine examples of traditional English Christmas cakes, one light and the other dark. They are recipes which have been treasured by the family of George H. Ford for many generations, and which Patricia Ford has very kindly shared with us.

You must begin your preparations the day before baking, as the fruit mixtures marinate overnight.

❧ WHITE CHRISTMAS CAKE

½ pound unsalted
  butter, softened
1 cup light brown sugar,
  packed
4 eggs, well beaten
1 pound golden raisins
  (approximately 3
  cups)
½ pound mixed candied
  peel (approximately
  1 cup)
¼ pound glacéed red
  cherries (approxi-
  mately ½ cup, packed)
½ pound blanched
  slivered almonds (scant
  2 cups)

One 8-ounce can crushed
  pineapple and juice
½ cup noncitrus fruit
  juice, such as pear,
  peach, apple
2 cups flour
½ teaspoon baking
  powder
½ teaspoon salt
¼ teaspoon mace
½ teaspoon vanilla
  extract

Cream the softened butter; add the sugar and beat until light. Add the beaten eggs and mix well. Combine with the raisins, mixed peel, cherries, almonds, crushed pineapple and its juice, and the ½ cup fruit juice. Let the mixture stand overnight in the refrigerator or a very cool place.

On the following day, preheat oven to 300°. Butter and flour two 8½-by-4½-inch loaf pans.

Sift the flour, baking powder, salt, and mace over the fruit mixture. Add the vanilla extract and combine all the ingredients well. Spread the batter evenly into the prepared loaf pans, and bake for 1 ¾ to 2 hours, or until a skewer inserted in the center of the cakes comes out clean. Cool thoroughly in the pans on a wire rack before unmolding.

This recipe may be doubled.

YIELD: TWO 2-POUND FRUIT CAKES

🎗 DARK CHRISTMAS CAKE

12 tablespoons (1½ sticks) unsalted butter, melted

5 eggs, well beaten

1 cup plus 2 tablespoons dark brown sugar, packed

1 pound golden raisins (approximately 3 cups)

1 pound dark seedless raisins (approximately 3 cups)

½ pound currants (approximately 1⅔ cups)

½ pound chopped dates (approximately 1 cup)

½ pound mixed candied peel (approximately 1 cup)

¼ pound glacéed red cherries (approximately ½ cup, packed)

2 ounces blanched slivered almonds (scant ½ cup)

2 ounces coarse-chopped walnuts (½ cup)

½ cup maple syrup

2½ cups flour

½ teaspoon baking soda

½ teaspoon allspice

½ teaspoon mace

½ cup brandy

¼ cup port wine

1 cup strawberry jam

Mix the melted butter, beaten eggs, brown sugar, fruit, nuts, and maple syrup in a large bowl and let stand overnight in the refrigerator or a very cool place.

On the following day, preheat oven to 300°. Butter and flour three 8½-by-4½-inch loaf pans.

Sift the flour, baking soda, allspice, and mace over the fruit mixture and combine. Mix in the brandy, port wine, and strawberry jam. Spread the batter evenly into the prepared loaf pans and bake for 1¾ to 2 hours, or until a skewer inserted in the center of the cakes comes out clean. Cool thoroughly in the pans on a wire rack before unmolding.

This recipe may be doubled.

YIELD: THREE 2-POUND FRUIT CAKES

COOKIES & SMALL CAKES

A N Y of the recipes in this chapter may be doubled.

❈ CHOCOLATE ALMOND THINS

*¼ pound unsalted
   butter, softened
½ cup sugar
1 egg
½ teaspoon almond
   extract*

*1 cup flour
1 cup ground blanched
   almonds*

FOR THE TOPPING
*3 ounces semisweet chocolate
1 ½ tablespoons unsalted butter*

Preheat oven to 350°.

Cream the butter and beat in the sugar gradually until the mixture is light. Beat in the egg and the almond extract. Fold in the flour and the ground almonds. Drop the batter by scant teaspoonfuls about 2 inches apart onto a lightly greased cookie sheet. Flatten into circles about ¼ inch thick. Bake for 12 to 15 minutes, or until very slightly browned around the edges. Cool a few minutes on the baking sheet and then remove with a spatula to a wire rack.

TO MAKE THE TOPPING

Melt the chocolate with the butter in the top of a double boiler over simmering water, stirring constantly. Drizzle the melted chocolate from a spoon over the cookies in a lined or random pattern.

YIELD: APPROXIMATELY
FIVE DOZEN COOKIES

〰 CHOCOLATE-COATED TILES

A bar cookie which is popular with children. It is a quick and practical recipe for bake sales.

FOR THE BATTER
½ pound unsalted butter, softened
⅔ cup sugar
2 egg yolks
1 teaspoon vanilla extract
1 cup flour

FOR THE TOPPING

6 ounces German's sweet baking chocolate
3 tablespoons unsalted butter
⅔ cup fine-chopped walnuts or pecans

Preheat oven to 350°. Butter a 10-by-14-inch pan.

Cream the butter and sugar until light and fluffy. Beat in the egg yolks and vanilla extract. Fold in the flour and spread the batter in the prepared pan. Bake for 15 minutes, or until the edges just begin to turn a pale brown. Cool thoroughly in the pan on a wire rack.

TO MAKE THE TOPPING

Melt the chocolate with the butter in the top of a double boiler over simmering water, stirring constantly. Spread while warm over the entire surface of the cake layer. Sprinkle with the chopped nuts and cut into 1¾-inch squares.

YIELD: FOUR DOZEN SQUARES

🎀 *CHOCOLATE GINGER TASSIES*

These small cookies have an unexpected ginger center topped with rich chocolate cream. They would go well with demitasse or an ice cream dessert. You may vary them by substituting orange or grapefruit marmalade for the ginger preserves. They keep very well.

FOR THE COOKIE DOUGH

6 tablespoons unsalted
  butter, softened
½ cup confectioners'
  sugar
1 egg yolk

½ teaspoon vanilla
  extract
1⅓ cups flour

Ginger preserves or
  marmalade

FOR THE CHOCOLATE FILLING

4 ounces German's sweet baking chocolate
4 tablespoons sugar
4 tablespoons heavy cream
½ teaspoon vanilla extract
2 tablespoons unsalted butter

TO MAKE THE COOKIES

Preheat oven to 350°.

Cream the butter and beat in the sugar. Add the egg yolk and vanilla extract, and then work in the flour. Form the dough into a ball. Pinch off small pieces of dough (about as much as a rounded teaspoonful) and press into the bottom and halfway up the sides of ungreased miniature muffin pans. (Diameter at base is 1¼ inches.) The back of a bowl-shaped measuring spoon does a good job of this. Bake the shells for 10 to 15 minutes, or until very lightly browned. Let them cool for a few minutes, and then carefully lift the shells out of the pan to a wire rack to cool completely. Place about ¼ teaspoon ginger preserves in the center of each shell.

TO MAKE THE CHOCOLATE FILLING

Melt the chocolate and sugar in the top of a double boiler over hot, but not boiling, water. Stir in the cream, vanilla, and butter, and continue cooking gently for about 15 minutes, stirring frequently, until the sugar is completely melted and the mixture is very hot. Remove from the heat and let it cool to room temperature, but do not let it harden or become firm. Drop a teaspoonful into each cookie shell to fill completely and cover the ginger preserves. As it continues to cool, the chocolate topping will become firm and shiny.

YIELD: ABOUT 2 ½ DOZEN COOKIES

CHOCOLATE WEDDING CAKES

These little mounds are a chocolate version of the Orange Wedding Cakes on page 89. The two packaged together would make an attractive gift.

¼ pound unsalted
   butter, softened
6 tablespoons
   confectioners' sugar,
   plus additional for
   dusting
2 ounces unsweetened
   chocolate, melted
   and cooled

1 ½ teaspoons vanilla
   extract
1 cup sifted flour
½ cup fine-chopped
   pecans

Cream the softened butter and beat in the sugar gradually. Stir in the cooled, melted chocolate and the vanilla extract. Fold the sifted flour and the chopped pecans into the batter. Cover the mixing bowl and refrigerate several hours until the dough is firm.

Preheat oven to 325°.

Break off small pieces of dough and roll between the palms of your hands into small balls or shape into crescents. Place them about an inch apart on a lightly greased cookie sheet and bake for 15 minutes, or just until the cookies are dry in the center. Remove to a wire rack and sift confectioners' sugar over them while they are still warm.

YIELD: APPROXIMATELY 2½ DOZEN COOKIES

✖ CINNAMON BOWS

This flaky cookie is made from a pastry dough. It can be shaped into bows, pretzels, initials, or whatever shape you choose.

1 cup flour	4 tablespoons unsalted
½ teaspoon cinnamon	butter, chilled
2 tablespoons sugar,	2 tablespoons vegetable
plus additional for	shortening, chilled
dredging	2 to 3 tablespoons cold
Grated rind of 1	water
medium lemon	

Mix the flour with the cinnamon, sugar, and grated lemon rind. Cut in the butter and vegetable shortening with a pastry blender or mix rapidly with the tips of your fingers until all the ingredients are well integrated. Sprinkle the mixture with only as much cold water as is necessary to form a dough. Chill the dough several hours until it is firm enough to handle. Keep the remainder of the dough in the refrigerator while forming each cookie.

Preheat oven to 350°.

Pinch off a walnut-size piece of dough and roll it lightly on a board with the palms of your hands to form a very narrow rope, about ⅛ inch in diameter and about 8 inches long. Keep your hands clean to prevent the dough from sticking. Dredge lightly in sugar and shape the rope into a bow, or whatever shape you like, pressing any joints to seal. Place the cookies about an inch apart on ungreased cookie sheets and bake for 10 to 12 minutes, until very pale in color. Remove with a spatula while warm and cool on a wire rack.

YIELD: ABOUT THREE DOZEN COOKIES

✂ DREAM BARS

During exam periods, a college friend of ours used to receive care packages of assorted cookies which she shared with her fortunate friends. Dream Bars were our favorite, and they sustained us through long nights of study. We have thought of these cookies from time to time, and here, if memory serves, is a close approximation of them. They are composed of two layers: a cake layer on the bottom and a meringue with chocolate chips on top. It is best to avoid making meringues in humid weather. Store loosely covered, never airtight.

FOR THE CAKE LAYER

6 tablespoons unsalted
butter
⅓ cup sugar
1 egg yolk

½ teaspoon vanilla
extract
1½ cups flour

FOR THE MERINGUE LAYER

1 egg white
Pinch of salt
Pinch of cream of
tartar

½ cup sugar
½ teaspoon vanilla
extract
⅓ cup chocolate chips

TO MAKE THE CAKE LAYER

Preheat oven to 325°. Lightly butter an 8-inch-square cake pan.
    Cream the butter and beat in the sugar. Add the egg yolk and
vanilla extract and mix well. Fold in the flour. Spread evenly in
the prepared pan.

TO MAKE THE MERINGUE

Beat the egg white with the salt and cream of tartar until almost
stiff. Add the sugar gradually, then the vanilla, and beat until
stiff peaks form. Fold in the chocolate chips. Spread over the cake
layer and bake for 40 minutes, or until the meringue is dry. Cool
in the pan on a rack and cut carefully into bars with a serrated
knife.

YIELD: TWENTY BARS

VARIATION:

Fold ½ cup coarse-chopped walnuts into the meringue layer in
addition to, or instead of, the chocolate chips.

✖ FORTUNE COOKIES

These fortune cookies are crisp and flavorful. They are a versatile gift, since the messages can be written to suit any occasion, including children's parties. Once the cookies are baked, the fortunes must be put into place quickly, so be sure to write them and snip them into strips before beginning to prepare the cookies.

1 egg white
3 tablespoons sugar
1½ tablespoons cornstarch
1 tablespoon flour
1 tablespoon unsalted butter, melted
¼ teaspoon almond extract

⅛ teaspoon lemon extract
2 teaspoons water
12 fortunes, cut into strips about ½ inch wide and about 2 inches long

Preheat oven to 350°.

Break up the egg white with a fork. Mix the sugar, cornstarch, and flour and sift this mixture into the egg white. Stir to mix. Stir in the melted butter, then the flavorings and the water.

Don't try to bake more than four or five at a time. Drop by teaspoonfuls, 2 inches apart, onto a buttered baking sheet. Bake for 4 to 5 minutes, or until browned around the edges. When browned, remove from the oven and immediately remove one cookie with a spatula.

Hold it in the palm of your hand and place a fortune in the center. Fold the cookie gently in half. Wrap the cookie, fold down, over the handle of a wooden spoon. Fold the corners around the spoon to meet each other and press together. Slide off the spoon. Work quickly, since, as the cookies cool, they become brittle. If this should happen, put them back in the oven for a minute to soften. Repeat with the remaining cookies and batter.

YIELD: APPROXIMATELY ONE DOZEN COOKIES

✕ GERTRUD BLUE'S BROWNIES

These moist, bittersweet chocolate cakes, dusted with confectioners' sugar, are aristocrats among brownies.

3 squares unsweetened
   chocolate
¼ pound unsalted butter
2 eggs
1 cup sugar
1 teaspoon vanilla
   extract

½ cup flour
1 cup coarse-chopped
   pecans or walnuts,
   optional
Confectioners' sugar

Preheat oven to 400°.

Melt the chocolate and butter in the top of a double boiler over hot, not boiling, water, stirring. Reserve, allowing to cool.

Beat the eggs, add the sugar gradually, and continue beating for 5 to 6 minutes until thick and pale. Add the vanilla and the cooled melted chocolate mixture, stirring to combine. Fold in the flour, blending it thoroughly into the batter. Add the nuts, if desired. Spread the batter evenly in a well-buttered 8-inch-square pan and bake for no longer than 20 minutes. Start testing with a toothpick after 15 minutes; when the brownies are done, the toothpick should have a very moist crumb on it. Be careful not to overbake, as these brownies should be moist and creamy. Cool thoroughly in the pan on a wire rack before cutting. When cold, cut into sixteen squares and dust with confectioners' sugar.

YIELD: SIXTEEN 2-INCH SQUARES

⚘ KIFLI

This tender and flaky cookie is usually made at Christmastime. The recipe is from Eastern Europe and was given to us many years ago. You may use any jam or marmalade as a filling instead of the nut mixture.

2 cups flour
¼ teaspoon baking
    powder
⅛ teaspoon salt
½ cake yeast
8 tablespoons (¼
    pound) unsalted
    butter

2 tablespoons
    vegetable shortening
3 tablespoons sugar
2 egg yolks
½ cup sour cream

FOR THE FILLING
2 egg whites, beaten until frothy and combined with:
½ cup coarse-ground pecans
½ teaspoon vanilla extract
2 tablespoons sugar

FOR THE TOPPING
Confectioners' sugar

Preheat oven to 350°.

Sift the flour, baking powder, and salt into a bowl. Crumble in the ½ cake of yeast. Cream the butter and the shortening, adding the sugar gradually, until smooth. Beat in the flour mixture, then the egg yolks, and finally the sour cream. Let the dough stand at least 30 minutes. Roll out and cut into 2½- to 3-inch squares. Spread about 1 teaspoon filling on each square. Bring two opposite corners of the square into the center and press them gently to seal them. If necessary, dip your finger into water and moisten the corners to help seal them together. Place on an ungreased baking sheet and bake for 18 to 20 minutes or until lightly browned. Cool and sprinkle with confectioners' sugar.

YIELD: APPROXIMATELY FOUR DOZEN COOKIES

✄ LIME TEA CAKES

Cakelike crescents surrounding a tart lime filling which keep and freeze very well.

FOR THE FILLING
   1½ tablespoons unsalted butter
   ¼ cup sugar
   1 egg, lightly beaten
   Grated rind and juice of 1 medium lime

FOR THE DOUGH

2 cups flour
*2 teaspoons baking
    powder*
3 tablespoons sugar
*Grated rind of 1 small
    lime*

*4 tablespoons unsalted
    butter, chilled*
2 eggs, lightly beaten
2 tablespoons milk
Confectioners' sugar

TO MAKE THE FILLING

Melt the butter in the top of a double boiler over simmering water. Using a whisk, gradually beat in the sugar, then the egg, then the lime juice and rind. Cook, stirring with the whisk until thick, about 5 to 8 minutes. Set aside to cool while you make the dough.

TO MAKE THE DOUGH

Preheat oven to 400°.

Sift together the flour and the baking powder. Stir in the sugar, then the lime rind. With a pastry blender, cut in the butter until the mixture is crumbly. Add the eggs and the milk and stir slightly. Combine, using your hands if necessary, until the mixture is smooth.

Roll out with a rolling pin on floured waxed paper to a thickness of about ¼ inch. Cut out circles with a round cookie cutter approximately 3 inches in diameter. Place ½ teaspoon of the filling on one half of each circle. Fold the other half of the circle over the filling and crimp the edges to seal well. Place on an ungreased cookie sheet and bake for 15 minutes, or until lightly browned. Cool and sprinkle with confectioners' sugar.

YIELD: TWO DOZEN CAKES

⚭ LINZER CAKES

These cakes are an adaptation of the traditional Linzer torte, with a fragrant and pleasing blend of spices, almonds, and lemon. They make an attractive gift when packaged with the Orange Flower Cakes, page 88, which are similarly shaped, but a contrasting color.

1 cup flour
½ cup light brown sugar
⅛ teaspoon ground cloves
¼ teaspoon cinnamon
1 teaspoon fresh-grated lemon rind

2 teaspoons pulverized unblanched almonds
½ cup unsalted butter
1 egg yolk
1 teaspoon vanilla extract
½ cup red raspberry jam

Preheat oven to 350°. Grease and flour 1½ sets of miniature muffin tins.

Sift the flour into a bowl, and stir in the sugar, cloves, cinnamon, lemon rind, and almonds. Add the butter and, with a pastry blender, cut it in until the mixture is crumbly. With a fork, stir in the egg yolk and the vanilla. Form the dough into a ball, using your hands if necessary. Don't overmix. Place the dough on floured waxed paper and lightly tap it down with a rolling pin until it forms a sheet ½ inch thick. Cut out circles with a floured 1- to 1½-inch-round cookie cutter. Place each circle into the prepared muffin tins. Indent the top of each cake with your thumb and place ½ teaspoon of jam in each indentation. Bake for 15 to

20 minutes, or until brown around the edges. Cool completely on a wire rack before removing from the pan. Loosen gently with a knife and lift out.

YIELD: APPROXIMATELY 1 ½ DOZEN CAKES

✄ MISS ELIZABETH HOLAHAN'S FINE TEA WAFERS

This is a thin, delicate, and crisp cookie on which infinite variations may be worked. The coriander, combined with the other flavorings, gives it a distinctive taste.

*¼ pound unsalted
    butter, softened
⅓ cup sugar
1 egg
1 tablespoon coriander*

*1 tablespoon vanilla
    extract
Grated rind of 1 lemon
¾ cup sifted flour*

OPTIONAL GARNISH
Approximately 3 dozen pecan halves

Preheat oven to 350°.

Cream the butter and beat in the sugar gradually. Beat in the egg, and then add the coriander, vanilla, and grated lemon rind. Combine the batter with the sifted flour. Drop by rounded half-teaspoonfuls onto greased cookie sheets, at least 2 inches apart. Flatten each cookie with an ice cube and press a pecan half onto

the top of each if desired. Bake for 8 minutes, or until the edges
are very lightly browned. Remove with a spatula and cool on a
wire rack. Store loosely covered to retain crispness.
YIELD: APPROXIMATELY THREE DOZEN
COOKIES

VARIATIONS:

1. Omit the pecan garnish and add ½ to 1 cup of fine-chopped
nuts to the batter.
2. Omit the coriander, vanilla, and lemon rind and add to the
batter:

> *2 squares melted unsweetened chocolate*
> *Grated rind of 1 orange*
> *1 tablespoon orange liqueur*
> *Increase the sugar to ½ cup. Omit the pecan garnish.*
> *Add ½ to 1 cup fine-chopped black walnuts, if desired.*

✂ *MOCHA MERINGUES*

These meringues are not difficult, but they should be made on a
dry day. Store them in loosely covered containers.

> *4 ounces German's sweet baking chocolate*
> *4 teaspoons instant coffee powder*
> *2 egg whites*
> *⅛ teaspoon cream of tartar*
> *¾ cup confectioners' sugar*

Preheat oven to 350°. Butter and flour a large cookie sheet.

Melt the chocolate with the coffee in the top of a double boiler over barely simmering water, stirring constantly. Then remove it from the heat and allow it to cool to room temperature.

Beat the egg whites until frothy; add the cream of tartar and continue beating until they hold firm peaks. Add the sugar gradually and continue beating until the egg whites are stiff and glossy. Fold in the cooled, melted chocolate. Drop by scant teaspoonfuls 1½ inches apart onto the prepared cookie sheet. Bake for about 15 minutes, or *just* until the centers of the meringues are dry. While still warm, remove them carefully with a spatula from the baking sheet to a wire rack to cool. Store loosely covered.

YIELD: APPROXIMATELY 2½ DOZEN MERINGUES

NUT WAFERS

1 tablespoon unsalted
    butter, softened
1 cup light brown
    sugar
3 tablespoons pastry
    flour

Pinch of salt
1 cup fine-chopped
    walnuts
1 egg, lightly beaten

Preheat oven to 350°. Oil and flour a large cookie sheet.

Cream the butter and, with your fingers, mix in the sugar, flour, and salt. Stir in the walnuts and the beaten egg. Drop by half-teaspoonfuls onto the prepared cookie sheet, spacing the cookies at least 2 inches apart. Bake for 8 to 10 minutes, or until dry.

Let stand for a few seconds, but remove them from the sheet while still warm, or they will stick.

YIELD: 2 ½ TO 3 DOZEN COOKIES

VARIATION:

✖ *FLORENTINE NUT WAFERS*

Melt 2 ounces semisweet baking chocolate with 2 teaspoons unsalted butter in the top of a double boiler over hot, not boiling, water, stirring constantly. Drizzle the melted chocolate from the tip of a spoon over the baked and cooled cookies.

✖ *ORANGE FLOWER CAKES*

Symbolic of fertility, orange blossoms have traditionally been used as bridal flowers throughout Europe and the West since the time of the Crusades. Orange Flower Cakes, which are flavored with orange water, would therefore be an appropriate sweet to serve at a bridal shower or wedding party.

1 cup flour	*1 teaspoon orange*
⅓ cup sugar	*flower water*
½ cup unsalted butter	*½ cup orange*
1 egg yolk	*marmalade*

Preheat oven to 350°. Butter and flour 1 set of miniature muffin tins.

Sift the flour into a bowl. Stir in the sugar and mix well. With a pastry cutter, cut in the butter until it is crumbly. With a fork, stir in the egg yolk and the orange flower water. Combine into a ball, mixing with your fingers, if necessary. Don't overmix. Put the dough on floured waxed paper and lightly tap it down with a rolling pin into a sheet about ½ inch thick. Cut out circles with a floured 1- to 1½-inch-round cookie cutter. Place each circle in a prepared muffin tin. Indent each circle with your thumb and put ½ teaspoon of marmalade into each indentation. Bake for 15 to 20 minutes, or until golden around the edges. Cool completely on a wire rack before removing from the tins. Loosen gently with a knife and lift out.

YIELD: APPROXIMATELY ONE DOZEN CAKES

✖ *ORANGE WEDDING CAKES*

A delicately flavored and textured cookie, shaped into spheres or crescents.

¼ pound unsalted
butter, softened
¼ cup confectioners'
sugar, plus additional
for dusting
1 tablespoon orange
liqueur

2 teaspoons grated
orange rind
1 cup sifted flour
½ cup fine-chopped
walnuts or pecans

Cream the softened butter, beating in the sugar gradually. Stir in the orange liqueur and grated orange rind. Fold in the sifted flour and the chopped nuts. Chill at least 1 hour, or until the dough is firm.

Preheat oven to 350°.

Break off small pieces of the chilled dough and roll between the palms of your hands into small balls, or shape into crescents. Place about 1 inch apart on ungreased cookie sheets and bake for 15 minutes, or just until dry in the center. Dust with confectioners' sugar while warm and cool on a rack.

YIELD: APPROXIMATELY 2 ½ DOZEN COOKIES

✖ PETITS FOURS

If you like, you can make the icing in several smaller amounts, coloring each batch with a different flavor jelly.

FOR THE CAKE

Make one half the recipe for the white cake in the Mother's Day Cake (page 49), using the following measurements:

3 eggs
¼ cup plus 2
  tablespoons sugar
½ cup plus 2
  tablespoons flour
⅛ teaspoon salt

3 tablespoons unsalted
  butter, melted
1 teaspoon vanilla
  extract
Grated rind of ½
  lemon

FOR THE ICING

¼ cup milk
¼ cup jelly, melted
(grape, raspberry,
strawberry, mint,
strained orange
marmalade, or peach
preserves, depending
on the color you
want. If you use
mint jelly, stir in ½
teaspoon peppermint
extract.)

3 cups confectioners'
sugar

TO MAKE THE CAKE

Preheat oven to 350°.

Proceed as directed on page 51, using one 9-inch-square cake pan. Bake the cake for 20 to 25 minutes, or until a skewer inserted in the center comes out clean. Cool in the pan on a wire rack for 5 minutes. Run a knife around the pan to loosen the sides and invert onto the rack. Cool completely. Wrap in plastic wrap and freeze overnight.

The next day, remove the cake from the freezer and cut it into 36 pieces, each 1¼-inch square.

TO MAKE THE ICING

Place the milk and the jelly in the top of a double boiler over simmering water. Add the sugar and stir until smooth. The icing should be thin enough to pour but thick enough to adhere to the cake. If it is too thin, add more sugar; if too thick, add more milk. Place one petit four in the pan with the icing and spoon the icing over the top and sides. Slide a small fork under the cake and carefully lift it out. Gently place the cake onto a rack to dry. When dry, remove by sliding a spatula under the cake and carefully lifting it off the rack.

YIELD: THREE DOZEN PETITS FOURS

VARIATION:

✖ MARMALADE PETITS FOURS

Slice the cake carefully into two even layers after removing it from the freezer. Spread the bottom layer with marmalade and place the second layer on top, forming a sandwich. With a serrated knife, cut the cake into 36 pieces, each 1¼ inches square. Place each square on a wire rack over waxed paper. Prepare the icing as directed above, using strained marmalade as the jelly. Pour or spoon the warm icing over each petit four, taking care to coat the sides. This method uses more icing than dipping, but the surplus can be reused by scraping it off the waxed paper while still soft and rewarming it in the double boiler.

✖ SURPRISE CAKES

Both crunchy and chewy, these little cakes with fudgy centers will last several days in the cupboard. They travel and ship well, and are good gifts for a household with children.

2 cups flour
¼ teaspoon salt
1 teaspoon baking
   powder
½ cup unsalted butter
1 cup sugar

1 egg, lightly beaten
1 teaspoon vanilla
   extract
1 tablespoon sweetened
   condensed milk

FOR THE FILLING

¼ cup unsalted butter,
   softened
1 egg yolk
½ cup confectioners'
   sugar

⅓ cup unsweetened
   cocoa
¼ cup ground hazelnuts
1 tablespoon rum

FOR THE TOPPING

1 tablespoon fine-chopped hazelnuts mixed with
   1 tablespoon sugar

Preheat oven to 350°. Butter and flour 3 sets of miniature muffin tins.

Sift the flour, salt, and baking powder together. Cream the butter until soft. Beat in the sugar by tablespoonfuls and beat until smooth and pale yellow. Beat in the egg. Beat in the flour mixture ½ cup at a time. Beat in the vanilla and the condensed milk. Wrap in waxed paper and refrigerate approximately 20 minutes, or until just firm enough to roll. Meanwhile, make the filling.

With the back of a wooden spoon, mix the butter and egg yolk until combined and smooth. Stir in the sugar, then the cocoa, and then the nuts, making sure that each is thoroughly combined before adding the next. Stir in the rum and set aside. When the dough is firm, roll out on floured waxed paper to a thickness of about ¼ inch. Cut out circles with a 1- to 1½-inch-round cookie cutter. Take one circle of dough, place about ½ teaspoon filling in the center, and top with a second circle of dough. Seal the edges well all around so that none of the filling is exposed. Repeat with remaining dough and filling, placing each cake in the prepared muffin tins. Leftover dough can be rerolled. Flatten each cake with your finger and sprinkle with the topping mixture, pressing down slightly so that the topping doesn't fall off.

Bake for 10 to 12 minutes, or until puffed and browned. Cool completely in the tins on a wire rack. Loosen gently with a knife and lift out.

YIELD: APPROXIMATELY THREE DOZEN CAKES

Rolled Cookies

The following recipe for rolled cookie dough can be used to make cut-out cookies for any occasion: hearts for Valentine's Day, Easter chicks and bunnies, Thanksgiving turkeys, or the Chocolate Leaves and Apricot-filled Cookies in the recipes that follow. To make Christmas tree ornaments, poke a hole in the top of each cookie with a straw and decorate with sparkles before baking; or decorate with colored icing after baking.

7 tablespoons unsalted butter, softened
½ cup confectioners' sugar
1 egg yolk
Grated rind of 1 medium lemon
1⅓ cups flour

Cream the butter. Gradually beat in the confectioners' sugar. Beat in the egg yolk and add the grated lemon rind. Work in the flour, mixing with your hands to form a dough. Chill for several hours until firm.

Preheat oven to 350°. Lightly grease a large cookie sheet.

Roll out the dough on a floured board to a thickness of ⅛ inch. Cut out and place on the prepared cookie sheet. Bake for 8 to 10 minutes until dry, but do not brown. Cool on a wire rack.

YIELD: APPROXIMATELY THREE DOZEN COOKIES, 2 INCHES BY 3 INCHES

Note: Recipe may be doubled or tripled, but work with only a portion of the dough at a time, keeping the rest refrigerated.

✣ APRICOT-FILLED COOKIES

These are pretty round sandwich cookies, with the jam showing through a hole in the center of the top layer. The recipe may be varied by using different jams for the filling.

1 recipe for rolled cookie dough, above, chilled
Apricot jam
Confectioners' sugar for dusting

Preheat oven to 350°. Grease a large cookie sheet.

Roll out dough on a floured board to a thickness of ⅛ inch or less. Use a 1¾-inch crinkle-edge biscuit cutter to cut out rounds of dough. Use a ¾-inch cutter to make a hole in the center of half of the rounds. Spread jam on the bottom rounds. Place the donut-shaped circles on top and bake on the prepared cookie sheet for about 10 minutes. The tops should remain pale and the bottoms should be lightly browned. Dust with confectioners' sugar while warm.

YIELD: APPROXIMATELY 2½ DOZEN COOKIES

✖ CHOCOLATE LEAVES

1 recipe of rolled cookie dough, page 95, well chilled

FOR THE CHOCOLATE COATING
4 ounces German's sweet baking chocolate
1 tablespoon unsalted butter

Preheat oven to 350°. Lightly grease a large cookie sheet.

Cut leaf patterns out of cardboard, approximately 3 inches long and 2 inches wide.

Roll out half the cookie dough at a time to a thickness of ⅛ inch. Cut out the cookies and bake for 8 to 10 minutes on the prepared cookie sheet. The cookies should not brown. Cool on wire racks.

TO MAKE THE CHOCOLATE COATING

Break up the chocolate and place it in the top of a double boiler with the butter. Stir over barely simmering water until melted. Remove it from the heat and stir for 2 minutes to cool slightly. Using the blade of a knife, spread the underside of each leaf cookie with a coating of chocolate. The chocolate will harden when cool.

YIELD: APPROXIMATELY THREE DOZEN COOKIES

SWEET TARTS
& PIES

B A S I C pastry is simply a combination of flour and fat, held together by a small amount of liquid. Other ingredients can be added, such as sugar for sweetness, ground nuts for flavor and a more crumbly texture, citrus rind for flavor, or eggs for flavor and strength. But the basic ingredients of pastry remain flour, fat, and a liquid.

Unsalted butter gives the pastry a rich flavor and a golden color, but if used as the sole shortening, the dough can be difficult to roll out and can cause the crust to be denser than desirable. Vegetable shortening, with a higher fat content, produces a flaky texture, but is colorless and flavorless. It is useful when a mere casing for the filling is needed, but is too bland for most sweet tarts. A combination of unsalted butter and vegetable shortening, usually in a ratio of 2 to 1, results in a crust that is both flavorful and flaky. Margarine doesn't have the flavor of butter or the high fat content of vegetable shortening. The flavor of salted butter is inferior to that of unsalted, and we don't recommend using it. If you do use salted butter, however, eliminate any salt called for in the recipe.

All fat must be cold when added to the flour, and the combining must be done quickly. If the fat gets too warm, it toughens the crust. Bowls made of metal, glass, or pottery are colder than plastic, and therefore are preferred for mixing pastry. Be particularly cautious on warm days. Don't allow your hands to become too warm, and try to work even more quickly than usual. A cool, fast hand is one of the greatest assets in pastry making. Your fingertips are more sensitive than any utensil and are the best implement to use to gauge when a pastry is properly mixed.

Any liquid can be used to hold together the flour and fat. Water is the most common, but milk, cream, and even fruit juices can be substituted. Liquids with a high acid content, such as sour cream, lemon or orange juice, or vinegar produce a flakier crust. Remember, though, that the liquid is meant as a binding agent, and only the minimum amount necessary to hold the dough together should be used. The quantity may vary according to the humidity or the properties of the particular flour used, so add the liquid gradually. Of course, whichever you use, it must be cold.

Any flavoring added to the dough must be fresh. A bottled lemon or orange rind will do nothing for your pastry, whereas a small amount of freshly grated lemon rind adds a lovely flavor. If you are adding a liquid flavoring, combine it with the liquid that you will be using as a binder and add it at the end.

Pastry should always chill for several hours before rolling so that it can rest. It will then roll out without shrinking back, will be less sticky, and will hold its shape better while baking. The dough can be refrigerated for a day or two or frozen. Thaw completely before rolling.

We have read that it is best to roll out pastry on a marble slab. That may be, but we have never found it necessary to acquire one. We did buy a pastry cloth once, but found it to be more of a nuisance than an aid. A Formica counter top is cool, smooth, and adequate for pastry making. The simplest and most foolproof method for rolling out pastry that we have found is to place a large sheet of waxed paper on the counter top and sprinkle it with about 1 tablespoon of flour. Place the dough on top and flatten it by pressing down once or twice with the rolling pin. Sprinkle with a tablespoon or so of flour and lay another sheet of waxed paper on top. If the dough is too hard to roll, let it rest for about 15 minutes to soften slightly. Roll out by pressing firmly on the center of the ball of dough and rolling toward the edges. The bottom sheet of paper allows you to turn the whole pastry if any angle is awkward. When rolled to the right size, remove the top sheet of paper and invert the pie plate or flan ring, centered, over the pastry. Loosen the bottom sheet of waxed paper and invert everything so that the plate now rests, bottom side down, on the counter. Peel off the paper which is now on top. Press the pastry gently down into the plate and shape the sides as desired. For a tart, we usually make the sides a double thickness. It is stronger that way and also tastier. Freezing the pastry dough after shaping and before baking will result in a flakier crust. Fill or bake it directly from the freezer.

To bake a pastry "blind," or unfilled, prick the bottom and sides all over with a fork. Press lightly buttered aluminum foil into the center and up the sides of the unbaked pastry crust. Fill the foil with raw rice, beans, or peas, and bake at 375° for 20 minutes, or until dry. At this point, the crust is "partially baked." To make a "fully baked" crust, after removing the foil and the beans, bake for an additional 15 minutes, until the crust is lightly browned. Store the beans in a container; they can be used over and over again.

An unfilled pastry shell should be baked in the middle of the oven. A filled pastry shell should be baked in the bottom third of the oven. If the crust browns too fast while baking a filled tart or pie, cover the crust loosely with aluminum foil.

An unfilled crust should be cooled thoroughly before filling. A filled tart or pie should be cooled on a rack so that the bottom crust doesn't become soggy.

Recipes in this chapter designated as "pies" should be baked in pie pans. Recipes designated as "tarts" should be baked in a flan ring or a straight-sided, shallow tart pan.

If you are doubling any of the following pastry recipes it is easier to make them in two separate batches.

⚘ FLAKY PIE CRUST

This recipe is relatively easy to prepare and can be used for any of the recipes in this chapter, unless otherwise specified.

1½ cups flour	*3 tablespoons vegetable*
2 tablespoons sugar	*shortening, chilled*
Grated rind of 1 lemon	*2 to 3 tablespoons*
5 tablespoons unsalted	*cold water*
butter, chilled and	
cut up	

Mix the flour, sugar, and lemon rind. With the tips of your fingers or a pastry blender, cut in the butter and vegetable shortening.

Add just enough cold water to hold the mixture together. Knead a few turns and form into a ball. Wrap and refrigerate until firm enough to roll out.

YIELD: PASTRY FOR THE BOTTOM CRUST OF A 9-INCH PIE OR TART

℈ *RICH TART CRUST*

This crust is flavorful and cookielike. Although tender, it is strong enough to support any filling and travels extremely well.

½ cup unsalted butter
1 ½ cups sifted flour
2 tablespoons sugar
¼ teaspoon salt
3 tablespoons pulverized
blanched almonds

2 teaspoons grated fresh
lemon rind
1 egg
1 to 2 teaspoons cold
milk (as necessary)

Soften the butter slightly by tapping it with a rolling pin. Mix the flour, sugar, salt, pulverized almonds, and grated lemon rind in a large mixing bowl. Make a well in the center. Add the butter in slices to the well, then the egg. Make a paste of the butter and the egg with your fingers, then gradually incorporate the dry ingredients, working quickly so that the butter doesn't become greasy. Form the dough into a ball, adding the cold milk, if necessary, to hold it together. Wrap in waxed paper and chill for 2 hours or overnight, if possible. Roll out between two pieces of waxed paper sprinkled with flour.

YIELD: PASTRY FOR A 9- OR 10-INCH FLAN RING

✄ SOUR CREAM TART CRUST

This is a crumbly dough and can be difficult to roll out. It can be patched easily, however, so that breaks in the pastry during the rolling out should not be discouraging. You will be rewarded at the end by a pastry crust that is both flavorful and flaky.

1½ cups sifted flour
2 tablespoons sugar
¼ teaspoon salt
7 tablespoons unsalted butter, chilled

2 tablespoons vegetable shortening, chilled
2 to 3 tablespoons sour cream

Put the flour in a mixing bowl with the sugar and salt and stir lightly until combined. Add the butter and shortening in 1-tablespoon portions. With a pastry blender or with your hands, cut the shortening into the flour until the mixture is pebbly. Add 2 tablespoons of the sour cream and stir in lightly. Scrape the sides of the bowl and, with your hands, knead the dough gently until it holds together in a ball. If necessary, add the third tablespoon of sour cream. Don't overhandle. As soon as the mixture forms a ball, wrap it in waxed paper and chill 2 hours or overnight. Roll out between two pieces of floured waxed paper.

YIELD: PASTRY FOR THE BOTTOM CRUST OF A 9-INCH PIE OR TART

✕ *APPLE ALMOND TART*

This tart has a luscious almond custard filling covered by a circular pattern of apple slices. It is both pretty and portable.

> *1 partially baked 9-inch flaky pie crust, page 101*
> *1½ pounds McIntosh, Delicious, or Ida Red apples*
> *Grated rind and juice of 1 lemon*

FOR THE ALMOND FILLING
> *7 ounces almond paste, not marzipan*
> *1 tablespoon unsalted butter, softened*
> *1 tablespoon brandy*
> *1 egg, slightly beaten*
> *1 tablespoon flour*

FOR THE GLAZE
> *½ cup apple jelly*

Peel and core the apples and cut them into thin slices (approximately ⅛ inch thick). As you slice them, toss in a bowl with the
lemon juice.

TO MAKE THE FILLING

Knead the almond paste until smooth. Beat in the softened butter,
brandy, egg, and flour.

TO MAKE THE GLAZE

Melt the apple jelly in a small saucepan; then simmer a few minutes until it coats the back of a spoon. Brush the bottom of the

pastry shell with a thin coating of the hot glaze. Allow to cool and set.

Preheat oven to 375°.

Spoon the almond custard into the glazed pie shell and bake for 10 minutes, or just until the custard is set. Remove and allow to cool.

Drain the apples and toss with the grated lemon rind. Beginning at the outside edge of the tart, place the apple slices in concentric, overlapping circles, covering the entire surface of the custard filling. Set a second layer of apple slices over this. Apples should mound slightly in the center of the tart. Bake in the preheated oven for 30 to 40 minutes, until apples are quite soft. (Cover loosely with aluminum foil during the last 10 minutes of baking if either the crust or the apples begins to brown.)

Reheat the remaining apple glaze and brush it over the surface of the baked tart.

YIELD: ONE 9-INCH TART

CHOCOLATE FUDGE PIE

You will find that the walnut crust on this pie works equally well in other pie recipes, such as lemon or mocha chiffon. The filling is rich, moist, and very chocolatey. The recipe comes from Molly Stern, a woman whose artistic skill is reflected in her fine cuisine.

FOR THE WALNUT CRUST
  4 tablespoons unsalted butter, softened
  ¼ cup sugar
  1 tablespoon flour
  1 cup coarse-chopped walnuts

Note: Walnuts should be chopped by hand, as a blender or food processor will chop them too fine.

FOR THE CHOCOLATE FILLING

¼ pound unsalted butter, *⅓ cup flour*
 softened   *½ teaspoon baking*
1 cup sugar   *powder*
3 eggs, lightly beaten *⅛ teaspoon salt*
2 ounces unsweetened *1 teaspoon vanilla extract*
 chocolate, melted and
 cooled

Mix all the ingredients for the walnut crust and press into the bottom and halfway up the sides of a 9-inch pie pan.

Preheat oven to 325°.

Measure all the filling ingredients into a mixing bowl and mix until smooth. Pour into the walnut crust and bake for 35 to 45 minutes. The filling will rise above the level of the crust, and it should be slightly moist when done. The pie may be served as it is, or with very slightly sweetened whipped cream or vanilla ice cream.

YIELD: ONE 9-INCH PIE

❧ CHOCOLATE PECAN PIE

Pecans rise to the top, forming a delectable crust which covers the smooth, chocolatey filling. This must be made as a pie rather than a tart, since a tart crust is too shallow to contain the chocolate mixture. It is a pie, however, that is easy to transport and that keeps well for several days.

½ cup sugar	4 tablespoons unsalted
1 tablespoon flour	butter, melted
1 tablespoon unsweetened	1 teaspoon vanilla extract
cocoa	1 cup coarse-broken
3 eggs	pecans
1 cup light corn syrup	1 unbaked 9-inch Flaky Pie
	Crust, page 101.

Preheat oven to 350°.

Stir the sugar, flour, and cocoa together in a bowl to combine them. Beat the eggs lightly with a fork in a second bowl. Stir in the corn syrup, melted butter, and vanilla. Add the flour mixture and stir until well combined. Stir in the pecans.

Pour into the unbaked pie crust and bake for 50 to 60 minutes, or until the filling is firm.

YIELD: ONE 9-INCH PIE

✄ GREEN GRAPE TART

Whole green grapes, standing upright on a layer of slightly sweetened crème fraîche, stud the surface of this tart. The grapes are brushed with a clear glaze, giving them a crystalline appearance, and the entire effect is refreshing and summery.

Plan ahead, as it takes 1 to 2 days to make the crème fraîche.

FOR THE CRÈME FRAÎCHE
> *1 cup heavy cream*
> *⅓ cup sour cream, or 1½ teaspoons buttermilk*
> *1 to 1½ tablespoons light honey*

FOR THE GLAZE
> *½ cup apple jelly*

> *1 fully baked 9-inch pastry shell*
> *1 pound seedless green grapes, stemmed, washed, and dried*
> *Grated rind of 1 large lemon*

TO MAKE THE CRÈME FRAÎCHE

Place the heavy cream and the sour cream or buttermilk in a lidded glass jar and shake vigorously to blend. Unscrew the lid, cover loosely, and let stand in a warm place until the mixture is very thick. In hot weather this may take only half a day; in cold weather it could take 2 days. After the crème fraîche has been made, stir in 1 to 1½ tablespoons honey, according to taste.

TO MAKE THE GLAZE

Melt the apple jelly in a small saucepan and simmer for several minutes until it is slightly reduced and coats the back of a spoon. Brush a coating of hot jelly over the bottom of the baked pie shell and allow to set.

Spread the crème fraîche filling evenly over this and refrigerate until it is firm. Starting in the center of the tart, set the grapes upright in concentric circles on top of the filling, leaving a narrow band uncovered at the outside edge. Sprinkle the grated lemon peel over this band. Reheat the remaining glaze and brush over each grape. Keep refrigerated until ready to transport or serve.

YIELD: ONE 9-INCH TART

✕ KENTUCKY SWEET POTATO PIE

This tastes and looks very much like a pumpkin pie, but the bourbon gives it a distinctive flavor. It should be served with slightly sweetened, bourbon-flavored whipped cream on the side.

¾ cup light brown sugar　　*2 eggs*
1 tablespoon flour　　　　　*¾ cup heavy cream*
½ teaspoon cinnamon　　　　*¼ cup bourbon*
½ teaspoon nutmeg　　　　　*1 partially baked 9-inch*
¼ teaspoon salt　　　　　　　*Flaky Pie Crust,*
1⅓ cups puréed cooked　　　　*page 101*
　sweet potatoes, fresh or
　canned

FOR THE GARNISH
Approximately 12 pecan halves

Preheat oven to 375°.

Beat the brown sugar, flour, cinnamon, nutmeg, and salt into the puréed sweet potatoes. In another bowl, beat the eggs lightly and combine them with the cream and bourbon; stir this into the sweet potato mixture and mix well. Pour into the prepared pie shell and bake for 35 to 45 minutes, or until a knife inserted in the center of the pie comes out clean. Cool on a wire rack and garnish with pecan halves.

YIELD: ONE 9-INCH PIE

❧ *KIWI STRAWBERRY TART*

This is an exotic tart: rings of strawberries alternate with bright green kiwi fruit over a tart lime filling. It should be refrigerated if it is not served within a few hours after baking, and should therefore not be transported very far.

> *3 cups strawberries*
> *3 kiwi fruit*

FOR THE LIME CREAM FILLING

⅓ cup heavy cream	*½ cup sugar*
1 tablespoon flour	*4 egg yolks*
Grated rind and juice of	*3 tablespoons unsalted*
2 large limes	*butter, softened*

FOR THE GLAZE

> *½ cup apple jelly*
> *1 to 2 tablespoons kirsch*

> *One 9-inch fully baked pastry shell*

Wash and hull the strawberries and drain thoroughly on paper towels until dry. Peel the kiwi fruit and slice it crosswise into ¼-inch-thick pieces.

TO MAKE THE FILLING

Mix the cream and flour in the top of a double boiler, stirring with a wire whisk until smooth. Add the lime juice, lime rind, and sugar and cook over simmering water until very hot and thickened (5 to 7 minutes). Stir a little of the mixture into the egg yolks and then pour the yolks into the pan, stirring constantly. Continue to cook for approximately 5 minutes longer, stirring with a wire whisk until the custard is very thick, but do not let it boil. Remove from the heat and beat in the softened butter. Cover and cool.

TO MAKE THE GLAZE

Melt the apple jelly in a small saucepan over low heat. Stir in the kirsch and simmer 5 to 8 minutes until the jelly coats the back of a spoon and is slightly reduced. Use while hot.

Paint a thin coating of glaze over the bottom of the baked pastry shell. Allow to set. Spread the cooled lime cream filling over this. Starting at the outside edge of the tart, set a row of strawberries upright around the circumference. Alternate with a row of kiwi slices laid flat. Continue in this manner until the tart is covered, ending with a large strawberry in the center. Reheat the remaining glaze (if it has set) and brush it over the fruit.

YIELD: ONE 9-INCH TART

✕ LIME TART

Both tangy and sweet, this tart has a refreshing quality that is very pleasing. The pale green custard is garnished with shimmering glazed lime slices. The lime filling can be made several days in advance and refrigerated until needed.

4½ tablespoons unsalted butter
1 cup sugar
3 eggs
Grated rind and juice of 3 medium limes
1 fully baked 9-inch Rich Tart Crust, page 102

FOR THE GARNISH

½ cup sugar
¼ cup water
¼ cup fresh lime juice (lemon juice can be substituted)
1 lime, sliced thin

Melt the butter in the top of a double boiler over simmering water. Gradually beat in the sugar with a whisk. Beat in the eggs, then the lime juice and rind. Cook, stirring, until thick, about 8 minutes. Cool completely. Pour into the prebaked tart crust and smooth the top.

TO PREPARE THE GARNISH

Place the sugar, water, and juice in a small saucepan and boil gently about 15 to 20 minutes until a syrup forms. Add the lime slices and simmer 5 to 10 minutes until they are nicely glazed. Don't let them fall apart. Remove them gently with a fork and drain on a rack until completely dry. Depending on the humidity, this could take over an hour. When dry, slit each slice once from the outside rind just past the center core. Spread the cut corners away from each other and lay on the lime filling so that the rind is on top, forming an S shape. Arrange the slices around the crust in a circular design, with one in the center.

YIELD: ONE 9-INCH TART

✂ NECTARINE CUSTARD TART

We went on many picnics as children, but among the ones re-membered most fondly were those that began with fried chicken and tomato and basil salad and ended with a very special peach custard pie. We have altered the pie slightly by using nectarines instead of peaches, but it still remains special and is capable of conjuring up images of lazy days with the late afternoon light spreading across the grass.

4 to 5 nectarines, ripe but not soft
1 unbaked 9-inch Sour Cream Tart Crust, page 103

1 cup sugar
2 tablespoons flour
2 eggs
2 tablespoons unsalted butter, melted

Preheat oven to 350°.

Dip the nectarines into boiling water for 30 seconds. This makes them easier to peel. Peel each nectarine. With a paring knife, cut around the circumference of each nectarine and pull it apart gently from the stem depression. Remove each pit. Place each nectarine half in the palm of your hand, stoned side down, and slice it into 5 to 6 horizontal slices. Place one of the halves in the center of the unbaked tart crust and the rest around the outside of the crust. The end result should be a circle of sliced nectarine halves, with one in the center.

Mix the sugar and flour together with a fork. Break up the eggs with a fork. Add the melted butter to the eggs and stir just to mix. Stir in the sugar and flour mixture. Don't beat. Stir just enough to blend all the ingredients.

Pour the custard over the nectarines. Bake for 45 to 50 minutes, or until the custard is set and slightly browned. It should have an attractively browned crust on top.

YIELD: ONE 9-INCH TART

VARIATION:

Apricot halves, unsliced and unpeeled, offer a slightly different texture and color, but are also good.

✖ ORANGE CHOCOLATE TART

The smooth, rich flavor of the chocolate contrasts with the tartness of the oranges. At the same time, the chocolate provides a buffer zone so that the oranges don't cause the crust to become soggy. Thus, this tart is more portable than most orange tarts.

5 oranges
1 cup orange juice
1 cup sugar
1 tablespoon Cointreau
2 teaspoons orange flower water

FOR THE FILLING

4 ounces German's sweet
baking chocolate
4 tablespoons sugar
4 tablespoons heavy cream

½ teaspoon vanilla
extract
2 tablespoons unsalted
butter

1 fully baked 9-inch Rich
Tart Crust, page 102,
made with orange rind
rather than lemon rind

FOR THE TOPPING
Reserved orange syrup
½ ounce unsweetened chocolate

Peel the oranges and cut them into thick round slices. Combine the juice, sugar, Cointreau, and orange flower water in a saucepan over low heat. Stir until the sugar dissolves. Raise heat and boil, stirring, until it reaches the consistency of a syrup, about 15 to 20 minutes. Add the orange slices and cook about 10 minutes until the oranges are nicely glazed, but don't let them cook so long that they fall apart. Remove with a slotted spoon and drain well on a rack. They must be completely dry. Reserve the syrup.

TO PREPARE THE FILLING

Melt the chocolate and the sugar in the top of a double boiler over hot, but not boiling, water. Stir in the cream, vanilla, and butter, and continue cooking gently for about 15 minutes, stirring frequently, until the sugar is completely melted and the mixture is very hot. Remove from the heat and let cool to room temperature, but do not let the chocolate harden or become firm. Spread the prebaked tart crust with the chocolate and let it stand until set. Arrange the dried glazed orange slices on top of the chocolate.

TO MAKE THE TOPPING

Boil down the syrup until it is as thick as melted jelly and brush it over the oranges as a glaze. Grate the chocolate on top of the finished tart.

YIELD: ONE 9-INCH TART

VARIATION:

Bananas instead of oranges are a simple and delicious variation. Arrange banana slices over the chocolate. Glaze the bananas with a simple apricot glaze (page 117).

✖ PEAR CHOCOLATE TART

4 to 6 pears, ripe but not
  soft, preferably Bosc
2 cups white wine
1 cup sugar
One 1-inch piece vanilla
  bean
1 cinnamon stick

1 tablespoon lemon juice
6 ounces semisweet
  chocolate
2 tablespoons unsalted
  butter
1 fully baked 9-inch Rich
  Tart Crust, page 102

FOR THE GLAZE AND TOPPING
½ cup apricot preserves
2 tablespoons brandy
*¼ cup toasted sliced almonds or chopped unsalted
   pistachios*

Peel and halve the pears, removing the stems. Combine the wine, sugar, vanilla bean, cinnamon stick, and lemon juice in a saucepan large enough to hold all the pears. Heat until the sugar is dissolved. Add the pears and simmer gently until they are tender but not soft. Cool in the syrup and then core.

Melt the chocolate in a double boiler. Add the butter and stir until smooth. Cool until thick enough to spread. Spread the chocolate on the bottom of the prebaked tart crust and cool until hardened.

Place a pear half face down on the palm of your hand, and slice it into 5 to 6 horizontal slices. Place face down on the chocolate, spreading the slices slightly toward the center. Repeat with the remaining pear halves, arranging them in a radial design around the crust. Finish by placing one pear half in the center.

TO PREPARE THE GLAZE

Melt the preserves in a small pan and rub them through a strainer. Stir in the brandy. With a pastry brush, gently brush the glaze over each pear half.

Let the glaze set and sprinkle the finished tart with the almonds or pistachios.

YIELD: ONE 9-INCH TART

✕ PEAR CRANBERRY TART

This tart looks beautiful on a holiday table: pears are arranged in a radial design on a bed of dark red cranberry conserve. It is a refreshing close to a special dinner.

4 to 5 Bosc pears, ripe but
* not soft*
2 cups white wine
1 cup sugar
One 1-inch piece vanilla
* bean*
1 tablespoon fresh lemon
* juice*

Slivered rind of 1 orange
1 cup Cranberry Orange
* Conserve or Cranberry*
* Pear Chutney (page*
* 160 or 165)*
1 fully baked 9-inch Rich
* Tart Crust, page 102*

FOR THE GLAZE AND TOPPING
½ cup apple jelly, melted
2 tablespoons Cointreau, or other orange liqueur
¼ cup walnuts , lightly toasted and chopped coarse

Wash, peel, and halve the pears, removing the stems. Combine the wine, sugar, vanilla bean, lemon juice, and orange rind in a saucepan large enough to hold all the pear halves. Heat until the sugar is dissolved. Raise the heat to medium, add the pears, and simmer gently until tender. Don't overcook them; they should hold their shape. Cool in the syrup and then core.

Spread the cranberry conserve on the bottom of the prebaked tart crust. Place a pear half face down in the palm of your hand and slice it into 5 to 6 horizontal slices. Place face down on the conserve, spreading the slices slightly toward the center. Repeat with the remaining pear halves, arranging them in a radial design around the crust. Finish by placing one pear half in the center.

TO PREPARE THE GLAZE AND TOPPING

Combine the melted apple jelly and the Cointreau. Let cool until it thickens slightly. Gently brush glaze over each pear half. Let set, then sprinkle the toasted walnuts on top.

YIELD: ONE 9-INCH TART

VARIATION:

Use 1½ cups Pear Mincemeat, page 161, instead of the Cranberry Orange Conserve.

✹ PLUM-WALNUT CREAM TART

This is a pleasant way to celebrate autumn's bounty. The plums bake into a deep reddish purple and their tartness contrasts with the sweetness of the walnut cream surrounding them.

1 tablespoon light honey
1 tablespoon fresh lemon juice
1 tablespoon apple brandy
12 to 14 prune plums, washed and dried

FOR THE FILLING

¾ cup unsalted butter
¾ cup sugar
2 whole eggs
2 egg yolks

2 tablespoons apple
brandy
2 tablespoons sour cream
¾ cup pulverized walnuts

One 9-inch unbaked Sour
  Cream Tart Crust,
  page 103
2 tablespoons walnuts,
  broken up

Preheat oven to 350°.

Mix together the honey, lemon juice, and brandy in a mixing bowl large enough to hold all the plums. Find the seam of each plum and cut along this seam around the circumference of each plum. Place your thumbs in the stem depression and pull each plum in half. They should come apart easily. Remove the pit. As each plum is prepared, put the halves into the bowl containing the honey mixture. Stir them occasionally to be certain that each plum is well coated.

TO MAKE THE FILLING

Cream the butter and sugar. Beat in the eggs and egg yolks one at a time, then the brandy, and then the sour cream. Stir in the walnuts.

Spread the walnut cream filling on top of the unbaked tart crust. Arrange the marinated plum halves, skin side down, in concentric circles on top of the walnut cream. Place the plums close together because they shrink while baking. Spoon any extra marinade into the plum cavities, trying not to let it spill over into the cream. Sprinkle the entire tart with the walnuts. Bake for 45 minutes, or until the custard is set and the edges of the crust are browned. YIELD: ONE 9-INCH TART

✖ STRAWBERRY ALMOND TART

3 egg yolks	4 teaspoons kirsch
½ cup sugar	One 9-inch Rich Tart Crust,
6 tablespoons unsalted	partially baked, page
butter	102
½ cup pulverized	1 quart strawberries
blanched almonds	

FOR THE GLAZE AND TOPPING
  ½ cup apricot preserves
  1 tablespoon kirsch
  ¼ cup sliced blanched almonds, slightly toasted

Preheat oven to 350°.

Beat the egg yolks and ¼ cup of the sugar until they form a ribbon. In a separate bowl beat the remaining ¼ cup sugar and the butter until smooth. Combine the butter mixture with the egg yolk mixture and stir until smooth. Stir in the pulverized almonds, then the kirsch. Pour into the partially baked tart crust. Bake for approximately 10 minutes, or until the cream is set. Watch closely so that the surface doesn't burn. Cool completely.

Wash and hull the strawberries and place them, stem side down, on paper toweling until they are completely dry, at least

20 minutes. When dry, arrange the berries, stem side down, in a circular pattern on top of the almond cream. Try to make a symmetrical pattern, with the smaller berries rimming the edge of the crust and the larger berries in the center.

TO PREPARE THE GLAZE

Melt the preserves in a pan and rub them through a strainer. Stir in the kirsch. With a pastry brush carefully glaze each berry. Let set, then sprinkle entire tart with the blanched almonds.

YIELD: ONE 9-INCH TART

CONFECTIONS

P L A C E a glass of water in the refrigerator before you begin to make candy. You will need it to help you gauge when the candy is done. The following guide should help you decide when your candy is ready:

Temperature	Stage	Description
230°–234°	Thread	Syrup forms a wispy thread when a small amount is dropped from a spoon into a glass of ice water.
234°–240°	Soft Ball	Syrup forms a soft ball which can be flattened between the fingers and almost dissolved after dropping a small amount into a glass of ice water.

Temperature	Stage	Description
244°–248°	Firm Ball	Syrup forms a ball which still keeps its shape when rubbed between the fingers after a small amount is dropped into a glass of ice water.
250°–266°	Hard Ball	Syrup forms a very hard, yet still pliable, ball after a small amount is dropped into a glass of ice water.
270°–290°	Soft Crack	Syrup forms very definite threads which are hard, but not yet brittle, when a small amount is dropped into a glass of ice water.
300°–310°	Hard Crack	Syrup forms hard, brittle threads immediately when a small amount is dropped into a glass of ice water.

One can confirm this with a candy thermometer, although it can be difficult to get an accurate reading when making small amounts. If you use a candy thermometer, buy a good one and take care of it to ensure its accuracy. A good candy thermometer should have a sliding clasp so that you can attach it to the side of the pan at more than one angle. That way it can be used with any amount of liquid. The thermometer should be submerged as far as it can go without touching the bottom of the pan. All candy thermometers have the different stages written on them. Bend down when you are reading the thermometer so that you read it at eye level. An inaccurate reading of even a few degrees can ruin a candy. If you are new at candy making, stand near the thermometer and check it frequently. As you become more experienced, you will be able to judge the approximate time that it will take to reach a certain stage.

Candy making requires careful attention. Don't try to turn the heat off under a syrup while you answer the telephone and then return 15 minutes later. The syrup will have hardened by the time you return and will never recover its original consistency.

When cooking a sugar syrup, wash down the sides of the pan frequently with a brush dipped in cool water. This prevents sugar crystals from forming and keeps the syrup or candy from crystallizing at a later date.

Use only pure ingredients. Be particularly careful with chocolate. As the price of chocolate has soared, imitations have flooded the market. Chocolate "flavored" does not mean pure chocolate. Even chocolate chips that are made with "real" chocolate contain additional ingredients which change its taste and its properties. Read labels carefully and be certain that you are using what you think you are.

When melting pure chocolate, stir it continuously. If you stop, the chocolate may separate and it will be streaked with gray after hardening. If you are flavoring the chocolate with any liquid, add it at the beginning. Don't add it after the chocolate has begun to melt, or it will harden instantly.

Melt all chocolate in a double boiler. Pure chocolate burns very quickly, and it is almost impossible to ensure a gentle enough heat without using a double boiler. Don't allow the water to touch the bottom of the upper pan, and don't allow the steam to escape into the pan containing the chocolate. It could cause the chocolate to harden.

It is difficult to attain a shiny finish on home-dipped chocolates, and they will never have the high gloss of commercially dipped candies. However, you will have more success if you control the temperature of the melted chocolate and the atmosphere of your kitchen. Do not work on a humid day. The ideal room temperature should be approximately 65 degrees. The temperature of the melted chocolate should be between 83 and 85 degrees. It is possible to maintain this temperature by keeping the chocolate in a double boiler over warm water as you are dipping.

Candy making can be a highly technical skill requiring years of practice. This section does not include those candies which require a specialized technique. We have included only those confections which are relatively simple to make and yet are of a high qualtiy.

All recipes, except the Candied Grapefruit Peel, can be doubled. All the dessert sauces should be kept under refrigeration and will last at least 2 weeks.

✄ CANDIED GRAPEFRUIT
OR ORANGE PEEL

Candied citrus peel can be made at your leisure and stored indefinitely in the freezer. We always have a batch of this tart-sweet confection on hand to bring to friends when invited to dinner. It must be watched very carefully during the final stages of cooking, but you should find the results well worth the extra effort. Do not attempt to cook more than one batch at a time.

4 grapefruit or 6 to 7 Florida oranges
3 cups sugar, plus additional for dredging
¼ cup light corn syrup
1½ cups water

Extract the juice or fruit from the grapefruit or oranges and reserve for another use. Clean the skins of any remaining pulp and stringy membranes, but leave the white inner skin intact. Cut into strips or wedge shapes, ⅜ to ½ inch wide. Immerse in a very large pot of water and boil for 10 minutes. Drain, immerse in fresh water, and boil again for 10 minutes. Repeat this a third time and drain.

Meanwhile, combine the 3 cups of sugar with the corn syrup and the water in a very heavy pan, about 4-quart size, and boil for 20 to 30 minutes, or until a medium syrup forms. Stir in the drained fruit peel and simmer for about 30 minutes or longer until the syrup becomes quite thick. Finally, simmer very gently, stirring constantly for about 15 minutes, or until most of the syrup has been absorbed by the peel and the peel no longer has a watery, acrid taste. You cannot watch it too carefully during the final stage of cooking: keep the heat low and stir to prevent scorching. If the syrup burns, it will caramelize, turning dark in color and imparting an unpleasant bitter taste to the candied peel.

Lay sheets of waxed paper on the counter and cover with sugar. Extract the peels with tongs, and strew them in the sugar, separating and coating each piece. Leave to dry for 24 hours. Store in plastic containers or covered jars. They will keep for long periods of time in the refrigerator and indefinitely in the freezer.

YIELD: APPROXIMATELY SIX CUPS

VARIATION:

For chocolate coating, melt 4 ounces German's sweet baking chocolate and 1 tablespoon unsalted butter in the top of a double boiler over simmering water, stirring constantly. Remove from the heat and stir for 2 minutes to cool slightly. Dip one end of each sugared peel in the chocolate and dry on wire racks.

✂ CHOCOLATE DISKS

These are simple to make and can be varied merely be changing the flavoring.

4 ounces pure chocolate, either semisweet or milk
2 teaspoons vegetable shortening
1 recipe flavoring of choice (see below)

Place chocolate and shortening in the top of a double boiler over barely simmering water. Stir as the chocolate melts and incorporates the shortening. Remove the entire double boiler from the heat just before the chocolate is completely smooth. Continue stirring over the hot water, but off the flame, until the mixture is smooth and silken. Immediately stir in the flavoring. Drop by spoonfuls onto waxed paper, smoothing each candy into a neat round. Cool until hardened. Carefully remove from the waxed paper and store in a cool, dry place. Do not refrigerate.

Flavorings: Use one of the following combinations:

1. *1 teaspoon instant coffee powder*
   2 tablespoons whole nuts, unsalted (pecans, cashews, almonds)
2. *1 teaspoon dried grated orange rind*
   2 tablespoons raisins
3. *1 tablespoon slivered blanched almonds*
   1 tablespoon grated coconut
4. *1 tablespoon candied cherries, chopped*
   1 tablespoon candied pineapple, chopped
5. *2 tablespoons almond brickle chips*

YIELD: ONE DOZEN CANDIES

✄ CHOCOLATE EASTER EGGS

Based on the traditional coconut cream Easter egg, these are superior to any of the commercial varieties. We think that the bitter chocolate is a perfect foil for the sweet filling.

4 ounces cream cheese
1⅓ cups confectioners' sugar
1 teaspoon vanilla extract
1 teaspoon almond extract
⅔ cup shredded coconut

FOR THE COATING

4 ounces unsweetened chocolate
3 tablespoons confectioners' sugar
1 tablespoon unsalted butter

Mix the cream cheese and the sugar in a bowl with a wooden spoon. Stir in the vanilla and almond extracts. When completely blended, stir in the coconut. Chill until firm.

TO MAKE THE COATING

Melt the chocolate and the sugar in the top of a double boiler over simmering water. Stir, and when almost completely melted, add the butter and stir until smooth. Remove from the heat and stir 2 to 3 minutes as the chocolate cools slightly.

Take a spoonful of filling and shape it into an egg shape. The filling is somewhat sticky, so don't try for a perfectly smooth egg. The unevenness, when coated with chocolate, is attractive. Dip the shaped filling into the chocolate. Turn it gently and remove it with a fork. (A fondue fork works nicely.) Let the excess

chocolate drip off; then lay the egg on waxed paper. Repeat with the remaining candy. Allow the eggs to harden 4 hours, or overnight. Store in a cool, dry place.
YIELD: APPROXIMATELY
TWO DOZEN CANDIES

✖ CHOCOLATE FUDGE

This is a good, firm-textured fudge with a bittersweet chocolate flavor. We like this recipe because the sweetness can be controlled by the amount of cocoa you add. If you do not mind a sweet fudge, however, you may use the basic fudge recipe, omitting the cocoa, to make any flavor you like, using 1 or 2 teaspoons of extract, such as vanilla, almond, lemon, etc. Or, you may vary the chocolate fudge recipe by adding to it ½ cup chopped nuts or raisins, or the grated rind of an orange, or a few teaspoons of liqueur, such as Cointreau or crème de menthe.

We do not advise using a candy thermometer to test for the "soft ball" stage, as the quantity of fudge is too small to register the temperature accurately. Have a glass of ice-cold water on hand for testing.

2 cups sugar
¼ cup fresh whole milk
¼ cup evaporated milk
¼ pound unsalted butter,
  cut into pieces

1 teaspoon vanilla extract
10 tablespoons unsweet-
  ened cocoa

Put the sugar, fresh milk, and evaporated milk into a heavy 1-quart saucepan (preferably enameled iron) and stir over low heat until the sugar melts. Bring to a boil and add the butter. Keep the mixture at a low boil, stirring constantly with a wooden spoon until it reaches the "soft ball" stage. (This will take about 5 to 7 minutes.) Remove the fudge from the heat while testing. Drop a half-teaspoonful into ice-cold water. If it can be formed into a soft, malleable ball with the fingers, it has cooked to the proper temperature. Take care not to overcook, or the fudge will become hard and granular after cooling. Remove from the heat and stir in the vanilla and cocoa. Beat the fudge constantly with a wooden spoon for several minutes, until it becomes very thick and firm. Spread it in a lightly greased 8-inch-square pan and cut into squares when cool.

YIELD: ABOUT ONE POUND

VARIATION:

✂ MOCHA FUDGE

Follow recipe above, but use only 8 tablespoons of cocoa and stir in along with it 1 tablespoon instant coffee powder dissolved in 2 teaspoons hot water.

✂ CHOCOLATE MINT WAFERS

These candies are after-dinner mints.

> *4 ounces pure dark sweet chocolate (German's, for*
> *example)*
> *1 tablespoon light cream*
> *1 teaspoon instant coffee powder*
> *6 drops peppermint oil*

Place the chocolate and the cream in the top of a double boiler over simmering water. Stir until the chocolate is melted and smooth. Stir in the coffee, then the peppermint oil. Pour 1 teaspoon of candy onto waxed paper. Immediately spread it with the back of a spoon or a spatula into a flat circle. Make the candies as thin and as flat as possible. Repeat with the remaining chocolate. Cool until hardened. Gently peel the waxed paper from the wafers. Go slowly, since they are fragile.

YIELD: APPROXIMATELY 1 ½ DOZEN CANDIES

✕ CHOCOLATE TRUFFLES

These are pure chocolate truffles—dark, smooth, and very chocolatey. If you should be able to keep them from eager fingers, they will keep up to a month in the refrigerator.

>   8 ounces German's sweet baking chocolate
>   ⅔ cup heavy cream
>   1 ½ tablespoons brandy
>   2 tablespoons unsalted butter, at room temperature
>   3 to 4 tablespoons unsweetened cocoa

Break the chocolate into small pieces and place in the top of a double boiler. Place over simmering water and heat, stirring, until the chocolate is melted and smooth. Place the cream in a separate pan over medium-high heat and bring to a boil, continuing to stir the chocolate while the cream heats. Watch the cream closely, and as soon as it begins to foam and boil, remove it from the heat and pour it all at once into the chocolate. Stir vigorously until the mixture is smooth. Stir in the brandy. Refrigerate 4 hours, or overnight.

Remove the chocolate mixture from the refrigerator. Cut the butter into slivers and drop them on the chocolate. With a whisk or a wooden spoon, gently beat until no traces of butter remain.

Form into rough, asymmetrical balls about 1 inch in diameter and roll in the cocoa. The truffles can be eaten cold or at room temperature.

YIELD: APPROXIMATELY FIVE TO SIX DOZEN CANDIES

VARIATION:

Add 2 tablespoons ground almonds to the mixture before rolling, and roll in additional nuts instead of cocoa.

COCOA-DUSTED MARZIPAN

You will find these simple and quick to make.

7 ounces almond paste, not marzipan
1 tablespoon kirschwasser or brandy, or 1 teaspoon rose
   water or orange flower water
½ to ¾ cup confectioners' sugar

FOR THE COATING
1 tablespoon unsweetened cocoa
1 tablespoon confectioners' sugar

Knead the almond paste until it is smooth and any lumps have disappeared. Mix in the kirschwasser or other flavoring; then gradually work in ½ to ¾ cup confectioners' sugar until the mixture is no longer sticky and is sweetened according to your own taste. Pinch off small pieces of marzipan and roll between the palms of your hands into balls ¾ inch in diameter.

TO MAKE THE COATING

Sift together the cocoa and confectioners' sugar. Roll each marzipan ball in the mixture until coated.

YIELD: APPROXIMATELY THIRTY CANDIES

VARIATION:

✕ CHOCOLATE-COATED MARZIPAN

Follow the recipe above, rolling the marzipan into small balls. Do not dust with cocoa. For the chocolate coating, melt 4 ounces German's sweet baking chocolate with 1 tablespoon unsalted butter in the top of a double boiler over barely simmering water, stirring constantly. Remove from the heat and stir for 2 minutes to cool slightly. Dip each marzipan ball in the chocolate, using your fingers, and turning to coat completely. Dry on a sheet of waxed paper.

✕ GLAZED SPICED NUTS

Pecans, almonds, and walnuts all work equally well. The nuts are surrounded by a brittle. These work better when the weather is cool, since in hot and humid weather they can become soft and slightly sticky.

½ cup water
½ cup sugar
⅓ cup light corn syrup
1 teaspoon ground
 cinnamon

¼ teaspoon ground
 cloves
¼ teaspoon ground
 allspice
1 cup nuts

Oil a cookie sheet generously with vegetable oil. Combine the water, sugar, and corn syrup in a saucepan and stir over medium heat until the sugar is dissolved. Raise heat to medium-high and add the cinnamon, cloves, and allspice. Boil gently until the syrup reaches the "hard crack" stage (300°) on a candy thermometer. Add the nuts and mix well, making certain that each nut is well coated. Remove clusters of nuts and glaze and place each cluster on the prepared cookie sheet. Cool until hardened, then lift off.
YIELD: APPROXIMATELY 1 ½ CUPS NUTS

PASTEL MINT PATTIES

1 tablespoon unsalted butter, slightly softened*
1½ tablespoons light corn syrup
1 cup plus 1 tablespoon confectioners' sugar, sifted**
5 drops peppermint oil
1 drop food coloring, optional

Blend the butter and corn syrup in a mixing bowl with the back of a wooden spoon. When thoroughly blended and smooth, add the sugar. It will look like there is too much sugar to blend with the

* Don't allow the butter to become so soft that it is oily.
** Measure the sugar by sifting it directly into a measuring cup and leveling it off with a knife or spatula.

butter and syrup, but don't despair. Mix with a spoon, scraping the sides of the bowl until most of the sugar is incorporated. Knead gently with your hands until the mixture has formed a smooth shiny ball. Knead in the peppermint oil and the food coloring, if desired. When the ball is uniformly colored, roll it into a long tube about ½ inch in diameter. Pull off a piece about ½ inch long and roll it between the palms of your hands to form a ball. Place on waxed paper and press down on the ball with the tines of a fork to form patties about 1 inch in diameter. Repeat with the remaining candy. Allow to dry in a cool dry place for at least 2 hours.

YIELD: APPROXIMATELY TWO DOZEN
1-INCH PATTIES

VARIATION:

COCOA MINT PATTIES

> *1 tablespoon unsalted butter*
> *2 tablespoons light corn syrup*
> *1 cup confectioners' sugar, sifted*
> *¼ cup unsweetened cocoa, sifted*
> *5 drops peppermint oil*

Follow the same procedure as above, adding the cocoa with the sugar.

ROSE PECANS

The glaze is a clear and bright brittle with a faint pinkish hue. As with the Glazed Spiced Nuts, page 134, these work much better when the weather is cool, since in hot, humid weather they can become slightly sticky.

½ cup water
½ cup sugar
One 1-inch piece
   vanilla bean
Grated rind of 1 lemon

6 dried rose hips
1 tablespoon dried
   hibiscus
1 cup pecans

Oil a cookie sheet generously with vegetable oil.

Combine the water and sugar in a saucepan and stir over medium heat until the sugar is dissolved. Add the vanilla bean, lemon rind, rose hips, and hibiscus and raise heat to medium high. Boil gently until the syrup reaches the "hard crack" stage (300°) on a candy thermometer. Remove the vanilla bean and the rose hips. Add the nuts and stir well, making certain that each nut is well coated. Remove clusters of nuts and glaze and place each cluster on the prepared cookie sheet. Cool until hardened. They can be lifted off easily when cool.

YIELD: APPROXIMATELY 1½ CUPS NUTS

✕ SUGARPLUMS

These are pretty, pleasantly tangy, and ship very well.

½ cup dried apricots
¼ cup dried apples
¼ cup golden raisins
½ cup pecans

¼ cup plus 1 tablespoon
   grated coconut
2 tablespoons kirsch
3 tablespoons sugar

Chop the apricots, apples, raisins, pecans, and coconut together by hand or in a food processor. All ingredients should be finely chopped and well blended. Add the kirsch and mix well to moisten. Form into balls about ¾ inch in diameter. Squeeze each ball slightly as it is being formed to be sure that it stays together. Roll each ball in the sugar. They keep for several weeks in an airtight tin and freeze well.

YIELD: APPROXIMATELY THREE DOZEN

SUGARED PECANS

2 cups pecans, whole
   pieces if possible
2 egg whites
½ cup sugar
2 teaspoons ground
   cinnamon
1 teaspoon any of the
   following: ground
   cloves, powdered
   allspice, ground
   nutmeg

¼ teaspoon either
   ground cardamom or
   ground ginger

Preheat oven to 350°. Lightly oil a baking sheet.

Place the nuts in a bowl with the egg whites and stir until each nut is thoroughly coated. Combine the sugar and spices in a second bowl. Remove the nuts from the egg whites with a fork and add them to the sugar. Stir until the nuts are well coated with the sugar-spice mixture. Pour them onto the baking sheet, separating them as you do so. Each nut should be separate. Bake for approximately 8 minutes, or until the nuts are browned and crisp. Cool 1 to 2 minutes and then remove with a spatula.

YIELD: APPROXIMATELY THREE CUPS NUTS

Dessert Sauces

✂ BUTTERSCOTCH SAUCE

Smooth and sweet, without being cloying, this bears no resemblance to the bottled variety.

¼ cup light corn syrup
½ cup light brown
* sugar*
2 tablespoons unsalted
* butter*

2 teaspoons fresh
* lemon juice*
2 teaspoons vanilla
* extract*
½ cup evaporated milk

Combine the corn syrup, brown sugar, butter, lemon juice, and vanilla in a small, heavy saucepan. Stir to blend and bring to a boil. Boil gently, stirring, for about 5 minutes, until the mixture is a very thick syrup. Remove from the heat and stir vigorously for 1 minute. Add half the evaporated milk and stir until combined. Set aside to cool. When cool, add the remaining evaporated milk and stir until combined. Be sure the sauce is absolutely smooth.

YIELD: APPROXIMATELY 1 ½ CUPS

〰 *CHOCOLATE SAUCE*

This chocolate sauce is fudgy, dark, and thick.

3 ounces unsweetened
chocolate
½ cup heavy cream
2 tablespoons milk
1½ teaspoons vanilla
extract
7 tablespoons sugar
1 tablespoon unsalted
butter

Flavoring: 1 to 2
teaspoons orange
liqueur, crème de
menthe, crème de
cacao, rum, or grated
rind of 1 orange,
optional

Put the chocolate, cream, milk, vanilla extract, and sugar in the top of a double boiler and melt it slowly over hot, not boiling, water, stirring constantly. Remove from the heat and stir in the butter, bit by bit, and any one of the flavorings, if desired.

This sauce will thicken as it cools. Keep it under refrigeration and return to room temperature or heat it gently in the top of a double boiler before serving.

YIELD: APPROXIMATELY ONE CUP

〰 *HARD SAUCE*

See page 65.

✂ MAPLE WALNUT SAUCE

Delicious on ice cream or poached fruit. It is important that only pure maple syrup be used.

> *1 cup maple syrup*
> *½ teaspoon fresh lemon juice*
> *2 teaspoons cornstarch dissolved in 2 tablespoons water*
> *1½ tablespoons rum*
> *¼ cup coarse-chopped walnuts*

Heat the maple syrup and lemon juice to boiling in a heavy saucepan. Add the cornstarch and water mixture and stir. Keep at a very low boil. If it begins to foam up, remove from the heat and stir it down. Simmer, stirring constantly, until the mixture thickens and becomes clear, about 5 minutes. A slight film will form on the bottom of the pan as you stir it. Add the rum and boil 1 minute. Remove from the heat and cool, stirring occasionally. When cool enough to touch, stir in the walnuts.

YIELD: 1 to 1½ CUPS

✂ ORANGE WALNUT SAUCE

This dessert sauce has a smooth, almost custardlike consistency and is not overly sweet. We use undiluted orange juice concentrate and add water separately to avoid cooking the orange juice itself, as cooking makes it bitter.

3/4 cup sugar
2 tablespoons
  cornstarch
1 1/3 cups water
2 teaspoons butter
6 tablespoons frozen
  orange juice
  concentrate,
  defrosted but not
  diluted

1 tablespoon plus 1
  teaspoon lemon juice
1/4 cup coarse-chopped
  walnuts
2 teaspoons
  Cointreau, optional

Measure the sugar and cornstarch into the top of a double boiler. Stir in the water. Bring the mixture to a boil over direct heat to thicken, then cook for 3 minutes, stirring constantly. Place over simmering water and continue cooking for 10 minutes, stirring occasionally. Remove from heat, cool slightly, and stir in the butter, orange juice concentrate, lemon juice, walnuts, and Cointreau, if desired.

YIELD: APPROXIMATELY TWO CUPS

✕ PEAR GINGER ICE CREAM SAUCE

See page 156.

PRESERVES

M A N Y people feel that putting up preserves is, at best, a risky endeavor. The greatest danger in home canning is the development of lethal botulism toxins. However, the preserves in this chapter are all made with high acid foods, in which the development of such toxins is extremely rare and likely to be impossible. Furthermore, they all have a high proportion of sugar which acts as a preservative. It is, therefore, the less hazardous forms of food spoilage caused by the growth of molds and yeasts that we are concerned with here. And we can assure you that if you follow carefully the instructions given below, you will eliminate that danger.

1. *Equipment you will need:*
    a) Jelly jars specifically manufactured for home canning. These have two-piece "dome" lids and screw bands and are sealed without paraffin.*

* It is not possible to seal foods which must be processed with paraffin, as the wax would melt during processing.

b) A large, wide-bottomed, heavy cooking kettle, preferably enameled cast iron.

c) Tongs to remove the jars and tops from hot water.

d) A ladle and a wide-necked funnel for filling the jars.

e) A water bath canner for processing the canned food: this is a large, deep kettle with a tight-fitting lid and a rack designed to hold the jars upright and stationary.

2. *Selection of fruit:*

Use only good, ripe fruit that is not overripe. Check for signs of spoilage and never use fruit that is soft or blemished. Wash all food carefully before preparing.

3. *Preparation of jars:*

Wash jars, lids, and bands in hot, soapy water. Rinse thoroughly and keep them immersed in hot water until you are ready to fill them. (Glass jars may crack if they are cold at the time you pour in hot preserves.) It is not necessary to sterilize them as this will be accomplished during processing. Follow the manufacturer's instructions for preparing the brand of lid you use. Some must be boiled, to temper, before using. It will simplify your preparations if you use only one brand. Examine all the jars for cracks or nicks in the rim and discard any that are damaged. Never use canning lids more than once; a seal cannot be guaranteed if reused. Screw-on bands may be reused if they are not rusted or bent.

4. *Cooking:*

Always use a large, heavy, wide-bottomed pot. Do not double the quantities given in the recipes. Watch the fruit carefully as it cooks, stirring when necessary to avoid scorching. Skim off any foam that appears on the surface. Cooking times given in each recipe are approximate. To test for proper consistency, remove the kettle from the heat, place a small amount of jelly or preserve on a cold saucer, and put it in the freezer compartment of your refrigerator for a few minutes. If it has jelled, bottle the preserves immediately. If not, simmer for a few minutes longer. If your recipe calls for pectin, read the instructions on the bottle of pectin and follow the cooking time specified in the individual recipe. As the pectin does the jelling, there is no need to test the consistency.

5. *Bottling:*

The food should be bottled as soon as it has cooked the requisite length of time. Use tongs to remove the jars from the hot water and set them on a clean dish towel. Ladle the hot preserves into the jars through a wide-necked funnel, filling to within ⅛ inch of the top for jellies and ½ inch for preserves, jams, and conserves. Wipe the rims and screw threads of the jars with a clean, damp cloth. If canning a thick substance, such as a conserve, run a clean, dull, nonserrated knife around the inside of the jar to eliminate any air bubbles. Remove the lids and bands from the hot water and place the lids squarely on top of each jar. Screw the bands on evenly and firmly, but do not use force to tighten.

6. *Processing:*

The United States Department of Agriculture and Cornell University now recommend that you process all jellies which are not clear, as well as jams, preserves, and conserves, in a water bath as described below, to prevent the growth of molds and yeasts which cause spoilage. Everything in this chapter must therefore be processed, and the requisite processing time is given with each recipe. Place the jars on the rack of the water bath canner as soon as they have been filled and sealed. Fill it with hot, but not boiling, water to a level 2 inches above the tops of the jars, leaving an additional 2-inch head space for boiling. Cover the canner with a tight-fitting lid and bring the water to a boil. Process for the length of time specified in your recipe, and do not begin timing until the water has reached a full boil. Maintain a full, steady boil during the entire processing time. If the water boils away, cover the jars with additional boiling water to keep them immersed.

7. *Storing:*

After processing, remove the jars from the canner with tongs and let them stand for 12 to 24 hours. Do not tighten the screw bands, or you may prevent a proper seal. If any lid appears to be domed, or slightly convex, press it with your finger. It should snap down flat. If it fails to do so, refrigerate it and use it as soon as possible. Remove the screw bands before storing, as they may trap moisture and become rusty if left on the jars. The lids will remain sealed without the bands. However, if you plan to send any preserves through the mail, it is advisable to replace the bands with fresh ones. To retain optimum quality, preserves should be stored in a cool, dry, and dark place.

If you are canning for the first time, you will be surprised to discover how easy it is, and you will undoubtedly feel proud of your accomplishment. But if you still feel uneasy about the prospect, you can always freeze preserves in plastic containers or freezing jars, rather than canning them. Just be sure to specify when giving them to friends that they must be kept under refrigeration.

Jellies

❧ ROSE PETAL JELLY

This rosy pink jelly is fragrant and delicately spiced. It is nice spread on toast or sweet breads and goes well with roast pork.

½ cup water
1½ cups dry white wine
2 cups sugar
1 cinnamon stick
1 tablespoon dried hibiscus, slightly crushed
12 dried rose hips, crushed
One 1-inch piece vanilla bean
12 cloves, slightly crushed

1 teaspoon cider vinegar
2 tablespoons lemon juice
½ teaspoon rose water or pure rose flavor
1 cup rose petals, pink or red, plucked from a bush or soon after falling, washed and dried
1 bottle liquid pectin
Cheesecloth

Prepare 4 half-pint jars according to the instructions in the introduction to this chapter.

Combine the water, wine, sugar, cinnamon stick, hibiscus, rose hips, vanilla bean, cloves, and vinegar in a saucepan. Heat slowly, stirring, until the sugar dissolves. Raise the heat and bring to a boil. Boil gently for 3 minutes. Strain through the cheesecloth and then return to the pan. Add the lemon juice, rose water, and rose petals. Bring to a boil and boil gently for 5 minutes. Quickly add the pectin. Keep the mixture at a rolling boil and stir constantly for 1 minute. Immediately pour into the prepared jars and seal according to the manufacturer's directions. Process 10 minutes in a water bath, according to the instructions in the introduction to this chapter.

YIELD: FOUR HALF-PINT JARS

✖ SAGE TRACKLEMENT

This herb jelly goes well with fowl and roast meats, particularly pork and lamb.

Grated rind of 1 lemon
3 cups apple cider
1 cup white wine
  vinegar
2 tablespoons lemon
  juice
4 cups sugar

⅔ cup fresh sage leaves,
  chopped and tightly
  packed
3 tablespoons dried leaf
  sage
1 bottle liquid pectin

Prepare 6 half-pint jars, lids, and bands according to the instructions in the introduction to this chapter.

Combine all the ingredients except the pectin in a large, heavy pot. Bring to a boil slowly, stirring occasionally, to dissolve the sugar. Allow the mixture to come to a rolling boil and then pour in the pectin all at once. Bring back to a boil and boil for 1 minute, stirring. Immediately pour into hot jars, seal, and process for 10 minutes in a water bath according to the instructions in the introduction to this chapter.

YIELD: SIX HALF-PINT JARS

✖ SWEET VIOLET JELLY

If you prefer to watch the profusion of violets in their natural setting, or if you miss the season altogether, use the synthetic flavoring sold in many spice departments. If lacking somewhat in authenticity, it has a bouquet and taste close to the original.

1 cup water
1½ cups dry white
  wine
1 tablespoon purple
  grape juice
3 cups sugar
Grated rind of 1 lemon
Two 1-inch pieces of
  vanilla bean
1½ teaspoons fresh-
  grated nutmeg

Juice of 1 lemon
1½ teaspoons almond
  extract
½ cup packed violet
  flowers, washed and
  dried, or ½ teaspoon
  violet essence or
  flavoring
1 bottle liquid pectin

Prepare 4 half-pint jars, lids, and bands according to the instructions in the introduction to this chapter.

Combine the water, wine, grape juice, sugar, lemon rind, vanilla bean, and nutmeg in a heavy saucepan. Cook, stirring, over low heat until sugar is dissolved. Raise the heat and bring to a boil. Boil gently for 10 minutes. Add the lemon juice, almond extract, and violets or violet essence. Return to a boil and boil gently for 5 minutes. Remove the vanilla bean. Add the pectin quickly, and bring back to a boil. Cook at a rolling boil, stirring, for 1 minute. Immediately pour into the prepared jars and seal according to the manufacturer's directions. Process in a water bath for 10 minutes according to the instructions in the introduction to this chapter.

YIELD: THREE TO FOUR HALF-PINT JARS

✖ TRUE MINT JELLY

Not cloying and with the true flavor of mint, this jelly does not dominate the flavor of lamb.

½ cup firm-packed fresh mint leaves, washed and dried
2 cups sugar
1 cup water

1 cup dry white wine
Grated rind and juice of 2 medium limes
1 bottle liquid pectin

Prepare 4 half-pint jars, lids, and bands according to the instructions in the introduction to this chapter.

Coarsely chop the mint leaves. Dissolve the sugar in the water and wine over low heat. Add the lime rind and juice and the chopped mint leaves. Raise the heat and bring to a boil. Boil 3 minutes. Pour in the pectin all at once. Bring to a rolling boil and stir for 1 minute. Immediately pour into the hot jars and seal according to the manufacturer's directions. Process for 10 minutes in a water bath according to the instructions in the introduction to this chapter.

YIELD: THREE TO FOUR HALF-PINT JARS

Preserves in Syrup

✂ CHESTNUTS IN BRANDY SYRUP

Serve on top of vanilla ice cream for *coupe aux marrons.*

2 to 2½ pounds chestnuts
3 cups sugar
1½ cups water
½ to ⅔ cup brandy

Prepare 5 half-pint jars, lids, and bands according to the instructions in the introduction to this chapter.

With a small, sharp knife, cut an X into the shell on the flat side of each chestnut. Place the chestnuts in a large saucepan of water to cover and boil for 15 to 20 minutes, or just until tender. Drain and peel off shells and skins while they are still warm.

In a large, heavy pot, boil the sugar and water for about 20 minutes, until a medium syrup is formed. Add the peeled chestnuts to the syrup and simmer for at least 1 hour. The liquid should be a caramel color and reduced by about one half, and the chestnuts will have absorbed some of the syrup. Ladle into the hot jars to within 1 inch of the top of the rim. Add 2 tablespoons brandy to each jar and seal. Process in a water bath for 15 minutes according to the instructions in the introduction to this chapter.

YIELD: FOUR TO FIVE HALF-PINT JARS

✺ BRANDIED PEACHES

¼ cup lemon juice
4 pounds peaches,
    preferably Freestone
    (approximately 15
    medium)
4 cups sugar
3 cups water

1 cup orange juice
Slivered rind of 1
    orange
1 cinnamon stick
One 1-inch piece vanilla
    bean
1 cup brandy

Prepare 4 one-pint canning jars, lids, and bands according to the instructions in the introduction to this chapter.

Put the lemon juice into a bowl large enough to hold the peaches. Dip the peaches into boiling water for 20 to 30 seconds and then peel with a paring knife. Find the seam that runs around the peach and slit around the peach on this seam with the paring knife. Place your thumbs on the stem depression at the top of the peach and gently pull it apart into two halves. Remove the pit and cut out the reddish center which surrounds it. Although harmless, it will discolor during the brandying process. Drop each peach half into the lemon juice, stirring to be certain that it is entirely coated with the juice. Repeat with the remaining peaches.

Dissolve the sugar in a large pot with the water and the orange juice over low heat. Add the slivered rind, cinnamon stick, and vanilla bean and raise heat. Boil, stirring occasionally, until a light syrup is formed. Add the peaches and any accumulated juices. Bring to a boil and boil gently for about 10 minutes. Be careful that the peaches don't become too soft. Ladle the peaches into the prepared jars and pour in enough syrup to come to within 1½ inches of the top of the jar. Pour in 1 inch of brandy and seal the jars according to the manufacturer's directions. Process for 20 minutes in a water bath according to the instructions in the introduction to this chapter. When completely sealed and cooled, turn the jar upside down gently once or twice to be certain that the brandy and syrup are mixed. Let the jars rest in a cool dark place a least one month before using.

YIELD: THREE TO FOUR 1-PINT JARS

✄ MINTED PEARS

The pears develop a refreshing flavor and aroma. Serve them with vanilla ice cream and chocolate sauce.

2 pounds Bartlett or Anjou pears, ripe but not soft (about 10 pears)	Cheesecloth
	3 cups sugar
	3 cups water
¼ cup lemon juice	Slivered rind of 1½ lemons
1½ cups firm-packed fresh mint leaves, washed and dried	2 tablespoons white crème de menthe or other mint liqueur

Prepare 4 one-pint jars, lids, and bands according to the instructions in the introduction to this chapter.

Peel, halve, and core the pears. As each half is prepared, put it in a bowl with the lemon juice. Stir to be certain that each is thoroughly coated with the lemon juice. Tie the mint leaves in a cheesecloth bag. This isn't absolutely necessary, but the mint leaves become unattractive after boiling and we prefer to remove them before canning.

Heat the sugar and water in a large pot until the sugar dissolves. Raise the heat and boil gently until a light syrup is formed, about 15 to 20 minutes. Add the pears and any accumulated liquid, the mint leaves, and the slivered rind. Return to a boil and simmer until the pears are tender, stirring occasionally. This should take about 10 to 20 minutes, depending on the ripeness of the pears. Remove the mint leaves. Add the liqueur and bring back to a boil. Immediately ladle into the prepared jars and seal according to the manufacturer's directions. Process for 20 minutes in a water bath according to the instructions in the introduction to this chapter.

YIELD: THREE TO FOUR 1-PINT JARS

Preserves

❧ BLUEBERRY JAM

5 *cups blueberries*
4 *cups sugar*
⅓ *cup lime juice* (*juice of 2 limes*)

Prepare 4 half-pint jars, lids, and bands according to the instructions in the introduction to this chapter.

Rinse the blueberries, discarding any that are soft or green and any stems. Place in a large, heavy pot with the sugar and lime juice and cook slowly until the sugar melts. Raise the heat and boil for 15 minutes, or until a candy thermometer reaches 210°. The jam will appear to have the consistency of a syrup, but it will thicken when cool. Test by putting a little on a saucer and chilling it in the freezer for a few minutes, and remove the jam from heat while testing. Pour into hot jars, seal, and process for 10 minutes in a water bath according to the instructions in the introduction to this chapter.

YIELD: FOUR HALF-PINT JARS

✕ PEAR GINGER JAM

An unusual jam, slightly accented with ginger.

4 pounds ripe Bartlett
    pears (about 8 cups,
    chopped)
½ cup lemon juice
4 teaspoons grated lemon
    rind

3 cups sugar
¼ cup light honey
¼ cup minced crystallized
    ginger (about 6 pieces)
1 cinnamon stick

Prepare 5 half-pint jars, lids, and bands according to the instructions in the introduction to this chapter.

Peel and core the pears and chop them into rather small pieces. Put them in a large, heavy pot with all the remaining ingredients.

Bring slowly to a boil and simmer, stirring frequently, for about 30 minutes. The mixture should look almost as thick as apple-sauce. Test by placing a small amount on a saucer and chilling it in the freezer for a few minutes, and remove the jam from the heat while testing. Remove the cinnamon stick and pack the jam into hot jars. Seal and process for 10 minutes in a water bath according to the instructions in the introduction to this chapter. YIELD: FIVE HALF-PINT JARS

VARIATION:

✖ PEAR GINGER ICE CREAM SAUCE

Follow the recipe above, but remove from the heat before the sauce becomes too thick. It should have the consistency of a syrup. Bottle and seal as for jam.

✖ SPICED PEACH JAM

4 pounds ripe peaches	*5 whole cloves*
(about 8 cups,	*One 2-inch piece*
chopped)	*vanilla bean*
4 cups sugar	*Cheesecloth*
⅔ cup lemon juice	*3 tablespoons brandy*
1 cinnamon stick	

Prepare 5 half-pint jars, lids, and bands according to the instructions in the introduction to this chapter.

Peel the peaches by immersing in boiling water for 20 to 30

seconds so that the skins will slip off easily. Chop them coarse and combine with the sugar and lemon juice in a large, heavy pot. Tie the cinnamon stick, cloves, and vanilla bean in a double thickness of cheesecloth and put it in with the peaches. Bring slowly to a boil and simmer for about 45 minutes, stirring frequently, until the syrup is as thick as honey. Test for jelling by placing a small amount on a saucer and putting it in the freezer for a few minutes until chilled. Remove the jam from the heat while testing. Stir in the brandy and simmer very briefly. Pack into hot jars, seal, and process for 10 minutes in a water bath according to the instructions in the introduction to this chapter. YIELD: FIVE HALF-PINT JARS

STRAWBERRY PRESERVES

5 cups strawberries, ripe but not soft
4 cups sugar
⅓ cup lemon juice
¼ cup kirsch

Prepare 5 half-pint jars, lids, and bands according to the instructions in the introduction to this chapter.

Wash and hull the berries. Let them stand, hulled side down, on paper toweling until dry. Put in a large stoneware pot with the sugar. Cover and let them stand overnight, stirring once or twice. The next day, slowly heat the berries until the sugar dissolves. Add the lemon juice, raise the heat, and boil gently about 15 to 20 minutes until thickened. Test by placing a small amount on a saucer and putting it in the freezer. Remove jam from the heat while testing. Skim the foam from the top. Stir in the kirsch. Immediately ladle into the hot jars and seal. Process in a water bath for 10 minutes according to the instructions in the introduction to this chapter.

YIELD: FIVE HALF-PINT JARS

Conserves

✖ APRICOT CONSERVE

Very sweet and rich, this goes well with roast pork or fowl. An added advantage is that it is made with dried apricots and you don't have to wait for the elusive apricot season.

1 ⅔ cups sugar
2 tablespoons light honey
½ cup fresh orange juice
1 ½ cups water
1 pound dried apricots (2 cups), chopped coarse
¼ cup raisins
1 thin-sliced lemon, including peel

¼ teaspoon cinnamon
½ cup slivered blanched almonds
½ teaspoon almond extract
¾ cup white rum

Prepare 5 half-pint jars, lids, and bands according to the instructions in the introduction to this chapter.

Dissolve the sugar and the honey in the orange juice and water

over low heat. Add the apricots, raisins, lemon slices, and cinnamon and raise the heat. Boil gently, stirring, for 15 minutes.
Add the nuts, extract, and rum. Return to a boil and boil gently
for an additional 5 minutes. Immediately ladle into the hot jars
and seal. Process in a water bath for 15 minutes according to
the instructions in the introduction to this chapter.
YIELD: FIVE   HALF-PINT   JARS

❯❮ BEET CONSERVE

This is an old Jewish recipe and is good with brisket of beef or
roast fowl. Store in a cool, dark place so that the beets will retain
their dark color.

2 cups raw beets (about 1½ pounds), peeled and diced	½ orange, sliced thin, including peel
1½ cups sugar	2 tablespoons crystallized ginger, minced
½ cup fresh orange juice	⅓ cup coarse-chopped walnuts
1 lemon, thin-sliced, including peel	¼ cup vodka, optional

Prepare 3 half-pint jars, lids, and bands according to the instructions in the introduction to this chapter.

Combine the diced beets, sugar, orange juice, sliced lemon, and
sliced orange in a heavy saucepan. Heat, stirring, until the sugar
is dissolved. Raise the heat and boil gently until the beets are
soft and the mixture is thick, stirring frequently. This will take
about 45 minutes. You can then see a glaze form on the beets
and the fruit. Add the ginger and the nuts and boil another 5

minutes. Add up to ¼ cup vodka, depending on how thick the mixture is. You don't want it to become too fluid. Pour into the hot jars and seal according to the manufacturer's directions. Process 20 minutes in a water bath according to the instructions in the introduction to this chapter.

YIELD: THREE HALF-PINT JARS

CRANBERRY ORANGE CONSERVE

The secret of this cranberry sauce is to cook the cranberries in orange juice instead of water. Other ingredients may be varied, if you wish, according to taste.

1 pound fresh
cranberries
2 cups sugar
2 cups orange juice
2 cups coarse-chopped,
peeled apples
½ cup golden raisins
¼ teaspoon allspice
¼ teaspoon ground
cloves

½ cup coarse-chopped
walnuts
¼ cup diced Candied
Grapefruit or
Orange Peel (page
126), or the grated
rind of 2 oranges

Prepare 5 half-pint jars, lids, and bands according to the instructions in the introduction to this chapter.

Wash the cranberries thoroughly, discarding stems and any soft berries. Put them in a large, heavy pot with the sugar and orange juice and cook until the skins begin to break (about 10 minutes). Add the chopped apples, the raisins, and spices and continue cooking, at a simmer, for 10 to 15 minutes, or until the sauce becomes thick. Skim any foam. Stir in the walnuts and the candied peel or grated rind during the last 5 minutes of cooking. Pack into hot jars, seal, and process 15 minutes in a water bath according to the instructions in the introduction to this chapter.

YIELD: FIVE HALF-PINT JARS

✄ PEAR MINCEMEAT

Homemade mincemeat is simple to prepare, and it is far better than the commercially canned variety. This recipe does not use either meat or suet, and can therefore be preserved in jelly jars, using the water bath method. Or, covered and stored in the refrigerator, it will keep for several months.

2 pounds firm Anjou or Bartlett pears, peeled, cored, and chopped coarse (about 4 cups)
1 medium apple, peeled, cored, and coarse-chopped
Grated rind and juice of 1 lemon
Grated rind and juice of 1 orange

1 cup dark seedless raisins
1 cup currants
1 cup light brown sugar
1 teaspoon cinnamon
1 teaspoon nutmeg
½ teaspoon allspice
¼ cup slivered almonds
3 tablespoons brandy

If the mincemeat is to be preserved, prepare 3 half-pint jars, lids, and bands, according to the instructions in the introduction to this chapter.

Place all the ingredients except the almonds and brandy in a large, heavy pot and simmer for about 45 minutes, or until fairly thick. Lower the heat and continue cooking, stirring occasionally to prevent sticking, for 20 to 25 minutes longer, or until very thick. Stir in the almonds and brandy during the last 5 minutes of cooking. If the mincemeat is to be preserved, pack it into hot jars, seal, and process in a water bath for 15 minutes according to the instructions in the introduction to this chapter.

YIELD: THREE HALF-PINT JARS, OR ENOUGH FOR TWO PEAR MINCEMEAT TARTS (SEE PAGE 119) OR ONE MINCEMEAT PIE

✂ PLUM CONSERVE

This goes well with turkey, goose, or any roast fowl.

24 fresh prune plums
(about 2 pounds),
washed and dried
1 cup dark raisins
1 thin-sliced orange
with peel, each slice
quartered

1 thin-sliced lemon
with peel, each slice
quartered
½ teaspoon cinnamon
3 cups sugar
1 cup walnuts or pecans,
broken up

Prepare 6 half-pint jars, lids, and bands according to the instructions in the introduction to this chapter.

Find the seam that runs lengthwise around each plum. Slice all the way around the seam and pull the plum in half gently from the stem end. If necessary, use your thumb to loosen the area around the pit. Remove the pits and chop the plums coarsely. Combine the chopped plums with the raisins, the orange and lemon slices, the cinnamon and the sugar in a heavy saucepan. Cook over medium-high heat, stirring, until thick, approximately 20 minutes. Stir in the nuts and cook, stirring, an additional 5 minutes. Pour into the hot jelly jars and seal according to the manufacturer's directions. Process for 15 minutes in a water bath according to the instructions in the introduction to this chapter.

YIELD: SIX HALF-PINT JARS

Chutneys

✖ *APPLE MINT CHUTNEY*

This goes well with lamb and curries.

*5 medium-sized crisp,
firm apples, such as
McIntosh or
Cortland, peeled,
cored, and coarse-
chopped (8 cups,
chopped)
1 ¼ cups packed fresh
mint leaves, washed,
dried, and chopped
coarse
1 cup dark seedless
raisins*

*¼ cup slivered lemon
rind
1 cup lemon juice
1 cup cider vinegar
1 ½ cups granulated
white sugar
½ cup light brown
sugar
3 teaspoons yellow
mustard seeds
1 large thin-sliced
yellow onion
2 teaspoons ground
ginger*

Prepare 6 half-pint jars, lids, and bands according to the instructions in the introduction to this chapter.

Combine all the ingredients in a large, heavy pot and simmer, stirring frequently, for 20 to 30 minutes, until thick. Pack into hot jars, seal, and process for 20 minutes in a water bath according to the instructions in the introduction to this chapter.

YIELD: SIX HALF-PINT JARS

CRANBERRY PEAR CHUTNEY

This is slightly tarter than the Cranberry Orange Conserve, page 160.

1 pound cranberries
⅓ cup dark raisins
1½ cups light brown
  sugar, packed
½ cup red wine vinegar
¼ cup lemon juice

Slivered rind of 1 lemon
4 firm pears (Bartlett
  or Anjou), peeled,
  cored, and chopped
  coarse (3 cups)

Prepare 5 half-pint jars, lids, and bands according to the instructions in the introduction of this chapter.

Wash the cranberries, removing stems and discarding any that are soft. Place all the ingredients except the pears in a large, heavy pot and simmer for 10 minutes. Add the chopped pears and continue simmering an additional 10 to 15 minutes, or until sauce is thick. Pack into hot jars, seal, and process 10 minutes in a water bath according to the instructions in the introduction to this chapter.

YIELD: FOUR TO FIVE HALF-PINT JARS

MANGO PAPAYA CHUTNEY

The tropical fruits used in this chutney are now available in most supermarkets during the summer months. The cultivated mangoes, however, are different in flavor from the wild "turpentine" mangoes used in Indian chutney, usually designated as "Major Grey's." Nor do they have the hard, fibrous texture of wild mangoes, so we recommend adding them during the latter part of cooking.

2 papayas, peeled,
    seeded, and chopped
    coarse (2 cups
    chopped)
½ cup dark seedless
    raisins
2 cloves garlic, crushed
2 cups light brown
    sugar, packed
½ cup granulated white
    sugar

¾ teaspoon allspice
½ teaspoon ginger
½ teaspoon nutmeg
Pinch of cardamom
2 cups cider vinegar
¼ cup lime juice
2 mangoes, peeled,
    pitted, and chopped
    coarse (2 cups,
    chopped)

Prepare 4 half-pint jars, lids, and bands according to the instructions in the introduction to this chapter.

Combine all ingredients except the mangoes in a large, heavy pot. Simmer 35 to 40 minutes, until the syrup begins to get thick and coats the back of a spoon. Add the mangoes and boil gently for 15 minutes longer. Pack into hot jars, seal, and process for 15 minutes in a water bath according to the instructions in the introduction to this chapter.

YIELD: FOUR HALF-PINT JARS

✗ QUINCE CHUTNEY

The quince is a rather hard, tart fruit, somewhat like a pineapple in flavor, but less sweet. It retains its firm texture after cooking like the wild mangoes used in Indian chutney.

*6 cups coarse-chopped
    quince, peeled, cored,
    and with all woody
    parts removed
⅓ cup dark seedless
    raisins
3 cloves garlic, crushed
1 tablespoon tamarind
    paste**

*½ teaspoon ground
    ginger
1 ½ cups dark brown
    sugar
1 cup red wine vinegar
    or cider vinegar*

Prepare 4 half-pint jars, lids, and bands according to the instructions in the introduction to this chapter.

Combine all ingredients in a large, heavy cooking pot. Simmer for 1 hour, or until sauce is thick, stirring toward the latter part of the cooking if there is danger of sticking. Pour into hot jars, seal, and process 15 minutes in a water bath according to the instructions in the introduction to this chapter.

YIELD: FOUR HALF-PINT JARS

* Tamarind paste is available in many ethnic food supply stores, such as Chinese, Middle Eastern, and Near Eastern.

✂ SECKEL PEAR CHUTNEY

1 cup granulated
  white sugar
¾ cup light brown
  sugar
1½ cups cider vinegar
4 cups tart apples,
  peeled, cored, and
  chopped coarse
  (McIntosh or Ida
  Reds do nicely)
8 cups Seckel pears,
  peeled, cored, and
  chopped coarse

½ cup dark seedless
  raisins
2 thin-sliced limes
Juice of 1 lime
2 teaspoons mustard
  seed
1 teaspoon ginger
2 cloves garlic, pressed
  or minced

Prepare 5 half-pint jars, lids, and bands according to the instructions in the introduction to this chapter.

Dissolve the sugars in the vinegar over low heat. Add the remaining ingredients and turn the heat up to medium. Simmer until the pears have softened, the mixture is thickened, and the flavors are well combined, about 25 minutes. Ladle into the hot jars and seal according to the manufacturer's directions. Process for 15 minutes in a water bath according to the instructions in the introduction to this chapter.

YIELD: FIVE HALF-PINT JARS

CONDIMENTS

T H E recipes in this chapter include seasoned vinegars, as well as savory sauces and flavored butters to serve with seafood and roast meat or fowl. Any of these recipes can be made in double or multiple quantities, as long as, when using a blender or food processor, you do not exceed the machine's capacity.

Vinegars

✻ HERBED RED WINE VINEGAR

*1 quart red wine
    vinegar
½ cup firm-packed fresh
    basil leaves, washed
    and dried, or 1½
    tablespoons dried
1 tablespoon fresh
    marjoram, washed
    and dried, or 1
    teaspoon dried*

*¼ cup fresh parsley,
    washed and dried
1 dried bay leaf
1½ tablespoons mustard
    seed
10 black peppercorns,
    cracked*

Combine all ingredients in a large bottle or crock. Seal with a screw top or cork and put in a cool, dark place for at least 2 weeks, or as long as 3 months. A basement shelf works well. Every few days for the first 2 weeks shake the bottle gently. After that, shake the bottle every 2 weeks. When ready to use, strain into clean bottles. If desired, place a small amount of herbs, preferably fresh ones, in each bottle. Close and label.

YIELD: ONE QUART

✂ BASIL VINEGAR

1 quart red wine vinegar
*1 cup firm-packed fresh basil leaves (or marjoram, or
dill), washed and dried*

Follow the same procedure as for Herbed Red Wine Vinegar.
YIELD: ONE QUART

✂ HERBED WHITE WINE VINEGAR

*1 quart white wine
vinegar*
*½ cup fresh parsley,
washed and dried*
*1 tablespoon fresh
thyme, washed and
dried, or 1 teaspoon
dried*
*1 tablespoon fresh
tarragon, washed and
dried, or 1 teaspoon
dried*

*1 tablespoon fresh
chives, chopped*
*1 tablespoon shallots,
peeled and crushed*
*1 garlic clove, peeled
and crushed*

Follow the same procedure as for Herbed Red Wine Vinegar,
page 170.
YIELD: ONE QUART

❧ LEMON MINT VINEGAR

1 quart cider vinegar
1 cup firm-packed fresh mint leaves, washed and dried
2 large strips lemon peel

Follow the same procedure as for Herbed Red Wine Vinegar, page 170.
YIELD: ONE QUART

❧ SAGE VINEGAR

1 quart white wine vinegar
1 cup firm-packed fresh sage leaves (or tarragon), washed and dried
1 tablespoon fresh savory, washed and dried, optional

Follow the same procedure as for Herbed Red Wine Vinegar, page 170.
YIELD: ONE QUART

Sauces

✖ *CAPER SAUCE*

This is an Italian sauce which has all the versatility of a green mayonnaise, but a more unusual and distinctive flavor. Serve it with poached or baked salmon, swordfish, or almost any seafood, or with roast meat. As a stuffing for cherry tomatoes, it makes a light summer hors d'oeuvre.

It is helpful to tie a card around a gift jar of caper sauce, suggesting its uses. It will keep for several weeks under refrigeration and freezes well. It should be served at room temperature.

1 cup parsley sprigs, packed
½ cup pignoli (pine nuts)
1 small jar capers (3¼ to 3½ ounces), well drained

½ slice white bread, crumbled and moistened in 2 tablespoons red wine vinegar
1 small garlic clove, peeled
½ cup olive oil

Purée all the ingredients except the olive oil in a blender or food processor. Then, with the motor running, slowly add the olive oil in a thin stream.

YIELD: ABOUT ONE CUP

✖ HERB AND CAPER MAYONNAISE

Delicately flavored with dill weed, parsley, and capers, this mayonnaise goes well with fish, chicken, or ham. It is made with ingredients which are easily obtained, but, if you have fresh herbs, you may substitute whatever combination you choose to make a unique gift from your own garden. Since mayonnaise spoils rapidly and should be kept under refrigeration, do not travel very far with it.

Ingredients should be at room temperature:

2 egg yolks	¼ teaspoon dried dill
1½ teaspoons Dijon	weed, or 1½ teaspoons
mustard	fresh
1 cup olive oil	4 teaspoons capers
1 tablespoon plus 1	Salt and fresh-ground
teaspoon fresh lemon	black pepper
juice	
2 tablespoons very fine-	
minced parsley,	
packed	

Beat the egg yolks with an electric mixer or wire whisk until light. Stir in the mustard. Add the olive oil drop by drop, beating constantly. After the mixture thickens, the rest of the oil may be added in a very thin stream. Stir in the lemon juice, parsley, dill weed, capers, and salt and pepper to taste.

YIELD: ABOUT 1 ¼ CUPS

❌ OTHELLO SAUCE

This is a piquant, light, and creamy sauce—and a remarkably versatile one. Combined with strips of poached chicken breast, it makes an elegant chicken salad. It is good on ripe garden tomatoes, on shrimp or other seafood, or as a cocktail dip for raw vegetables.

1 clove garlic, peeled
3 scallions, with most
of the green tops
¼ cup parsley sprigs,
packed
1 teaspoon
Worcestershire sauce

2 tablespoons white
wine vinegar
¾ cup mayonnaise,
preferably homemade
⅔ cup sour cream

Chop the garlic, scallions, and parsley in a blender or food processor. Add the Worcestershire sauce, vinegar, and mayonnaise and blend. Fold in the sour cream.
YIELD: 1 ½ CUPS

❌ PESTO

This is a highly aromatic sauce for pasta which originates in Genoa. It is particularly good with green fettucine, but can be used with any form of pasta. After the pasta has been cooked and drained, toss with pesto, which should be at room temperature, but not heated. You may not substitute dried basil for fresh in this recipe. Pesto may be frozen.

1 clove garlic, peeled
1 cup fresh basil leaves, packed
⅓ cup pignoli (pine nuts)*

⅔ cup fresh-grated Parmesan cheese
1 tablespoon unsalted butter
½ cup olive oil

Chop the garlic, basil leaves, and pignoli in a blender or food processor. Add the grated cheese and butter and blend. With the motor running, add the olive oil in a thin, steady stream.
YIELD: ABOUT 1½ CUPS

VARIATION:

✕ PARSLEY PESTO

This is a surprisingly successful alternative, and it can be made in any season, since fresh parsley is available in markets all year.

For the basil leaves in the recipe above, substitute 1 cup packed parsley sprigs. If available, you may also add about a dozen fresh mint leaves.

* Pignoli are always expensive and sometimes difficult to obtain. We've experimented with various other nuts and find the most successful substitution to be raw (not roasted or salted) cashews. They produce a coarser texture than pignoli, which are very soft, but the flavor is close.

✖ PROVENÇAL SAUCE

A piquant blend for any fish or seafood. Since it has a mayonnaise base and must be kept under refrigeration, do not travel very far with it.

2 *tablespoons fresh parsley, packed*	2 *egg yolks*
1 *small clove garlic, peeled*	¾ *cup olive oil*
	1 *tablespoon lemon juice*
1 *large shallot, peeled, or the white part of 1 scallion*	*Pinch of tarragon*
	Fresh-ground black pepper
5 *anchovy fillets*	1 *tablespoon capers*

Mince the parsley, garlic, shallot or scallion, and anchovies very fine, or mash with a mortar and pestle. Beat the egg yolks with an electric mixer or wire whisk in a small bowl until light, and then beat in the olive oil, drop by drop, increasing the flow of oil to a very thin stream as the mixture thickens. Stir in the lemon juice, tarragon, and the mixture of parsley, garlic, shallot, and anchovies. Add fresh-ground black pepper to taste, and fold in the capers.

YIELD: ABOUT ONE CUP

✖ TOMATO CHUTNEY

This is a different sort of chutney, not as sweet-sour as the usual because the tomatoes render their juice in cooking. It would go

very well with any baked or broiled fish or with roast chicken
or pork. It would also make a delicious pasta sauce, and for that
we recommend leaving out the cashews.

6 *cups peeled, coarse-*
*chopped tomatoes**
4 *cups peeled, coarse-*
chopped, and cored
apples
2 *medium yellow*
onions, sliced thin
1 *lemon, sliced thin*
6 *tablespoons slivered*
sweet green pepper
4 *tablespoons chopped*
fresh basil leaves, or
2 *teaspoons dried*

2 *teaspoons yellow*
mustard seed
1 *cup cider vinegar*
½ *cup white*
granulated sugar
½ *cup light brown*
sugar
½ *cup coarse-chopped*
raw cashews

Combine all the ingredients except the cashews in a large, heavy
cooking pot. Simmer for 30 to 45 minutes, stirring frequently,
until the sauce appears quite thick. Take care during the latter
part of cooking that it does not stick to the bottom of the pan.
Add the cashews during the last 5 minutes of cooking.

* Peel tomatoes by immersing in boiling water for 20 to 30 seconds so
that the skins will slip off easily.

Flavored Butters

The following are a few of our own suggestions for flavored butters. There are many possibilities, and you may improvise and experiment with blends of your own. If you have an herb garden, perhaps the best butter you can devise is one flavored with a mixture of fine-minced fresh herbs.

We use two methods in making flavored butters: cooking the butter with the ingredients for a more thorough blending of flavors, or whipping the butter and folding in the flavorings to preserve a lighter and creamier texture.

✂ *LEMON DILL BUTTER*

Serve this with baked or broiled fish.

> *4 teaspoons minced shallots*
> *1 tablespoon fresh dill weed, or ½ teaspoon dried*
> *4 teaspoons lemon juice*
> *6 tablespoons unsalted butter, softened*

Gently simmer the chopped shallots and dill weed in the lemon juice until most of the liquid has evaporated. Remove from the heat and cool to room temperature. Whip the butter until it is light and fluffy. Fold in the cooled shallot-dill mixture.

YIELD: ABOUT ½ CUP

❊ GREEN PEPPERCORN BUTTER

This is excellent with steak. Madagascar peppercorns packed in brine are the mildest and we prefer them.

> ¼ pound unsalted butter, softened
> 4 teaspoons green peppercorns
> 4 teaspoons brandy
> ½ teaspoon soy sauce
> 1 tablespoon chopped fresh tarragon, or ½ teaspoon dried

Whip the butter until it is light and fluffy. Crush the peppercorns; combine them with the brandy, soy sauce, and tarragon and simmer gently until most of the liquid is absorbed. Cool, then fold this mixture into the butter.

YIELD: ABOUT ½ CUP

❊ MUSTARD SHALLOT BUTTER

A cooked butter that is good with lamb chops.

> ¼ pound unsalted butter
> 1 tablespoon fine-chopped shallots
> 1 teaspoon Dijon mustard
> ⅛ teaspoon salt
> 1 tablespoon fine-chopped parsley
> Fresh-ground white pepper, to taste

Melt the butter in a small saucepan. While foamy, add the shallots and stir for 1 minute. Remove from the heat and add the remaining ingredients. Stir until the mustard is dissolved. Pour into a crock and chill. Before serving, bring to room temperature and stir to homogenize.

YIELD: APPROXIMATELY ¾ CUP

❧ CAPER BUTTER

This is good served with fish or as a spread with crackers.

¼ pound unsalted butter
1 tablespoon capers, drained
1 teaspoon minced green olives
1½ teaspoons drained and minced sweet pickles

Melt the butter in a small saucepan. Add the capers, olives, and pickles. Stir for 1 minute, mashing the capers slightly. Pour into a crock and chill. Before using, bring to room temperature and stir to homogenize.

YIELD: APPROXIMATELY ¾ CUP

SAVORIES

T H I S chapter includes hors d'oeuvre spreads and crackers, marinated vegetables, and spiced and salted nuts. Any of the recipes may be doubled.

❧ CAPONATA

A marinated eggplant and vegetable mixture, this makes a hearty summer salad, side dish, or hors d'oeuvre.

*1 large or 2 small
  eggplants
1½ cups diced raw celery
3 to 4 yellow onions,
  sliced
1 green pepper, sliced*

*1 sweet red pepper, sliced
Olive oil
¾ cup pitted black olives
½ cup pimiento-stuffed
  green olives*

3 tablespoons capers   2 tablespoons sugar
2 tablespoons pignoli   ⅓ cup red wine vinegar
  (pine nuts)   Salt and fresh-ground
1 to 1¼ cups tomato   black pepper
  purée

Dice the eggplant, sprinkle it heavily with salt, and let it drain in a colander for a few hours. Rinse thoroughly and dry. Parboil the celery and then sauté it with the sliced onions and peppers in a little olive oil until tender. Remove to a bowl, add more olive oil to the skillet, and sauté the eggplant until tender. Combine it with the sautéed celery, onions, and peppers. Add the black olives, green olives, capers, and pignoli. Combine 1 cup tomato purée, sugar, and vinegar and stir it into the caponata mixture. If it is too dry, stir in the remaining ¼ cup tomato purée. Add salt and fresh-ground black pepper to taste and chill before serving.

YIELD: ABOUT SIX CUPS

✂ CHOPPED CHICKEN LIVERS

The secret of this dish is in the preparation of the onions, which have a marvelous flavor, and in broiling the chicken livers, which then add no bitterness to the final product.

3 to 4 medium yellow onions
½ cup vegetable oil
½ pound chicken livers
4 hard-boiled eggs, peeled and quartered
¾ to 1 teaspoon salt

Slice the onions and fry in a *dry* frying pan, over a medium flame until they turn quite brown. Stir frequently. Be patient; this will take 20 to 30 minutes. Don't try to rush it or the onions will burn instead of brown. When brown, remove from the heat and pour the oil into the pan. Stir to coat the onions well. Let stand about 15 minutes.

Meanwhile, broil the chicken livers 5 minutes under a close flame, turning them once, until they are tender but no longer pink. Cool and cut into quarters, reserving any meat juices. In a large bowl, combine the quartered eggs, the livers, and any accumulated meat juices. Remove the onions with a slotted spoon and add them to the livers, reserving the oil. Chop the entire mixture by hand or in a food processor. If using a processor, turn it on and off frequently and don't overprocess. The final result should not be pasty or as smooth as a pâté. If you prefer not to have pieces of egg in the finished product, put the eggs in the processor first, and process for about 10 seconds. Then add the livers and onions. If the chopped livers seem too dry, add as much oil from the onion pan as necessary. Add ¾ teaspoon salt and mix well. Taste and, if necessary, add remaining ¼ teaspoon salt. Chill well before serving.

YIELD: APPROXIMATELY TWO CUPS

𝓧 CHOPPED CHICKEN LIVERS AND MUSHROOMS

This tastes best at room temperature and spread on small squares of thin-sliced white toast.

½ pound chicken livers
4 tablespoons unsalted
    butter
½ pound mushrooms,
    minced
4 scallions, with tender
    part of green ends,
    chopped
1 large clove garlic,
    peeled and crushed

1 tablespoon lemon juice
1 tablespoon plus 1 or 2
    teaspoons dry white
    wine
1 teaspoon Worcestershire
    sauce
Salt and fresh-ground
    black pepper

Simmer the chicken livers in water or chicken broth to cover in an enameled or stainless steel saucepan for 5 to 10 minutes, until cooked but slightly pink inside. Drain, cool, and chop fine.

Melt 2 tablespoons of the butter in a skillet. Add the minced mushrooms, scallions, and garlic and sauté over high heat for a few minutes. Add the lemon juice and 1 tablespoon of white wine and continue cooking until all the moisture has evaporated. Cool slightly, and combine with the 2 remaining tablespoons butter and the chopped livers. Add the Worcestershire sauce and salt and pepper to taste and moisten with 1 or 2 teaspoons additional white wine, if desired. Serve at room temperature.

YIELD: APPROXIMATELY ONE CUP

MARINATED MUSHROOMS

½ pound firm mushrooms, with the ends trimmed
¾ cup high-quality olive oil
2 garlic cloves, peeled and crushed
2 tablespoons coarse-chopped fresh parsley
Salt

Wipe mushrooms with a damp cloth to clean them. Slice them neatly. Place them in a ceramic or glass bowl. Combine the olive oil, garlic, and parsley. Pour over the mushrooms. Marinate, refrigerated, for 48 hours, stirring occasionally. After 48 hours, add salt to taste. Transfer to an attractive jar or crock to give as a gift. Instruct the recipient to keep them under refrigeration and to use them within two weeks.

YIELD: APPROXIMATELY 1½ CUPS

❧ *ROASTED PEPPERS*

8 large, thick sweet peppers, red or green, washed but not dried
2 cloves garlic, peeled and split
3 tablespoons olive oil

1 tablespoon coarse-chopped fresh basil, or ½ teaspoon dried
2 teaspoons wine vinegar, optional
Salt and pepper

Preheat oven to broil.

Place the peppers on a cookie sheet covered with aluminum foil 4 inches from the heat. Turn the peppers as the skins blister and blacken so that they will be evenly charred on all sides. This should take about 15 to 20 minutes. When all the skin has blistered, place the peppers in a brown paper bag. Close the bag tightly and let stand a minute or two so that steam forms in the bag. Remove the peppers one at a time and peel under cool running water. As each is peeled, place in a flat baking dish or in a wide-bottomed bowl.

Combine the garlic, oil, basil, vinegar (if desired), and salt and pepper to taste and pour over the peppers. Marinate for several hours, then cover and refrigerate.

YIELD: FOUR CUPS

✂ *SHRIMP BUTTER*

This is a good cocktail spread.

> *¼ pound unsalted butter*
> *One 7-ounce can tiny shrimp, drained*
> *½ teaspoon mace*
> *½ teaspoon fresh-ground nutmeg*
> *Fresh-ground white pepper*

Melt the butter in a saucepan. Add the shrimp and mash with a spoon until the shrimp and butter are well combined. Stir in the mace, nutmeg, and pepper to taste. Taste for seasoning. Pour into a crock and refrigerate. Before using, bring to room temperature and mix well.

YIELD: I ¼ CUPS

✂ *SMOKED SALMON SPREAD*

> *3 ounces cream cheese,*
> *softened*
> *2 tablespoons sour cream*
> *1 tablespoon drained*
> *prepared white*
> *horseradish*
>
> *2 to 3 teaspoons lemon*
> *juice*
> *¼ pound unsalted*
> *smoked salmon,*
> *shredded*
> *1 tablespoon capers*

Beat the cream cheese until light. Mix in the sour cream, horse-radish, and lemon juice to taste. Fold in the shredded salmon and the capers. Refrigerate until ready to use and bring to room temperature before serving.

YIELD: ½ CUP

❧ SMOKED TROUT SPREAD

*1 smoked trout filet
(approximately ¼
pound)
¼ cup sour cream
3 ounces cream cheese,
softened
2 tablespoons chopped
scallions*

*2 teaspoons drained
prepared white
horseradish
½ teaspoon lemon juice
6 pitted black olives,
halved*

Combine all ingredients except the olives in a bowl, mashing the trout slightly. Put into a crock or small bowl and decorate with the black olives. Refrigerate until ready to use. Serve cold or at room temperature.

YIELD: APPROXIMATELY ¾ CUP

❧ STILTON BUTTER

Serve on crackers as a cocktail spread.

*10 tablespoons unsalted butter, softened
6 ounces Stilton cheese
1 teaspoon Worcestershire sauce*

Whip the butter until it is light and fluffy. In a separate bowl, cream the Stilton cheese until it is smooth, then fold it into the whipped butter. Add the Worcestershire sauce and combine thoroughly. Refrigerate until ready to use and bring to room temperature before serving.

YIELD: ABOUT ¾ CUP

✂ *TARAMA SPREAD*

This is an unconventional *taramasalata* which includes sour cream. We find that it cuts the saltiness and produces a smoother spread.

1 small clove garlic,
 peeled
¼ cup parsley sprigs,
 packed
5 ounces tarama (carp
 roe)

8 slices white bread
2 tablespoons fresh lemon
 juice
1 cup olive oil
1 cup sour cream

Mince the garlic and parsley in a food processor or blender. Add the tarama and blend. Run the white bread, a few slices at a time, under tap water and squeeze out the excess moisture. Add them to the processor or blender and combine. With the motor running, add the lemon juice and the olive oil in a steady stream. Do not overblend or the mixture will become pasty. Turn into a mixing bowl and fold in the sour cream. Refrigerate until ready to use.

YIELD: ABOUT THREE CUPS

Nuts

❧ SPICED ALMONDS

Keep a supply of these on hand for unexpected guests or invitations. The oil prevents the almonds from darkening.

This recipe may be doubled, but if you do so, use a skillet large enough to hold the almonds in one layer. Also, add only 3 tablespoons oil and 1½ tablespoons seasoning, instead of doubling them.

> *2 tablespoons vegetable oil, preferably peanut oil*
> *1 cup blanched whole almonds*
> *1 tablespoon lemon-pepper seasoning*

Heat the oil in a heavy skillet large enough to hold the almonds in one layer. When the oil is hot, but not smoking, add the nuts and sauté until they are nicely toasted. Watch them carefully, and stir frequently to be sure that they do not burn. Drain on paper toweling. Put the spice mixture into a small brown paper bag. Don't use a plastic bag, because it will not absorb any excess oil. Add the drained nuts, twist the top to close, and shake the nuts and spices together. When the nuts are well coated, remove and put into containers.

YIELD: ONE CUP

❧ SPICED NUTS

These are good alone or with drinks. They make a good hostess gift since they are a complement to any kind of meal.

> *1½ tablespoons unsalted butter*
> *1 cup nuts (pecans, walnuts, Brazil nuts, or hazelnuts*
> *or a combination)*
> *1½ teaspoons coarse salt*

> *One of the following spice mixtures:*

> 1. *1 teaspoon powdered*
>   *ginger*
>   *½ teaspoon powdered*
>   *cloves*
>   *½ teaspoon ground*
>   *cinnamon*
> 2. *½ teaspoon powdered*
>   *allspice*
>   *½ teaspoon ground*
>   *nutmeg*
>   *¼ teaspoon ground*
>   *cinnamon*

> 3. *1½ teaspoons grated*
>   *orange rind*
>   *½ teaspoon cinnamon*

Heat the butter in a heavy skillet large enough to hold the nuts in one layer. When the butter begins to foam, add the nuts and sauté them quickly, stirring frequently. Regulate the heat so that the nuts will brown but the butter won't burn. When the nuts are well toasted, remove them from the pan with a slotted spoon and drain well on paper toweling. Add the salt and the spice mixture of your choice to a small paper bag. Add the nuts, twist the top to close, and shake the nuts and spices together. When the nuts are well coated, remove and put into containers.

YIELD: ONE CUP

VARIATION:

✺ SALTED NUTS

Add 1 teaspoon Worcestershire sauce to the butter as it is melting in the pan. Shake the nuts in the bag with salt only, no spices.

Crackers

✺ CHEDDAR THINS

These are flaky, crisp cocktail pastries which may be reheated before serving or eaten at room temperature. They are fragile and should be packed carefully.

> *1 cup extra sharp Cheddar cheese, grated (4 ounces)*
> *4 tablespoons unsalted butter, cut into small pieces*
> *1½ cups flour*

Place the grated cheese, butter, and flour in a mixing bowl and combine with a pastry blender or the tips of your fingers until a dough is formed. Knead for 1 or 2 turns and chill the dough until it is firm.

Preheat oven to 400°.

Roll out the dough, a third at a time, as thin as possible, on a floured board. Cut into strips 2 to 3 inches long and ¾ inch wide. Bake for about 5 minutes, watching to see that they do not brown. Store loosely covered.

YIELD: FIVE TO SIX DOZEN

VARIATION:

⚹ SWISS THINS

Follow the recipe above, substituting 1½ cups grated Swiss or Gruyère cheese for the 1 cup Cheddar. Sprinkle with grated Parmesan cheese before baking.

⚹ CHEESE BITS

These are crisp, Cheddar-flavored balls to eat with cocktails. They may be served at room temperature.

1 cup (24) ground Triscuits	*1½ teaspoons onion powder*
6 ounces extra sharp Cheddar cheese, grated	*1 teaspoon Worcestershire sauce*
1 cup flour	*¼ pound unsalted butter, cut into several pieces*

Preheat oven to 350°. Lightly grease a cookie sheet.

Place all the ingredients in a mixing bowl. Cut in the butter with a pastry blender until the mixture is crumbly and evenly mixed, but do not overwork the dough. Form into balls ¾ inch in diameter. Place on the prepared cookie sheet and bake for 10 to 12 minutes, or until dry in the center.

YIELD: APPROXIMATELY FIVE DOZEN

HERB PARMESAN BISCUITS

These savory biscuits may be served with cocktails or tea or as an accompaniment to soups. They should be stored in loosely covered containers, and may be served at room temperature or reheated briefly in the oven before serving.

1 cup flour
¼ pound unsalted butter, softened
1¼ cups fresh-grated Parmesan cheese
¾ teaspoon dried marjoram
¾ teaspoon oregano
¾ teaspoon dried basil
½ teaspoon Worcestershire sauce
2 to 3 tablespoons dry white wine

Place the flour, butter, cheese, and herbs in a mixing bowl. Cut in the butter with a pastry blender or the tips of your fingers. Moisten with Worcestershire sauce and just enough wine to form a dough. Roll into a log, about 1½ inches in diameter, and chill until firm.

Preheat oven to 400°.

Slice the chilled dough into rounds ¼ inch thick, place on an ungreased cookie sheet, and bake for 12 to 15 minutes, or until very lightly browned.

YIELD: ABOUT FOUR DOZEN

🙨 SESAME OAT CRACKERS

These coarse-grained crackers are easy to make and go well with soups, salads, and hors d'oeuvres. They would make a nice gift with one of the flavored butters or cocktail spreads.

1 cup flour	*¾ teaspoon salt*
¼ cup steel-cut oats	*½ teaspoon baking soda*
¼ cup cracked wheat	*½ cup buttermilk*
2 tablespoons sesame	*3 tablespoons unsalted*
seeds	*butter, melted*

Preheat oven to 350°. Lightly grease a baking sheet at least 10 by 13 inches.

Place all ingredients in a mixing bowl and combine thoroughly to form a dough. Knead briefly, divide the dough in half, and roll out each half separately on a floured board as thinly and evenly as possible. You should have a paper-thin rectangle approximately 10 inches by 13 inches. Place dough on the prepared baking sheet and pat it with your fingers to even it out. Prick the surface all over with a fork and score deeply with a knife into 2-inch squares, or whatever shape and size you like. Bake for 10 to 15 minutes, until thoroughly dry and very lightly browned. If outside squares brown more quickly, break them off and return the center section to the oven for a few minutes longer. Cool on a wire rack and break into sectioned squares. Store in loosely covered containers.

YIELD: APPROXIMATELY FIVE DOZEN
2-INCH SQUARES

VARIATION:

✖ CHEDDAR SESAME CRACKERS

Follow the directions for Sesame Oat Crackers, substituting the following ingredients:

1 cup flour
½ cup grated Cheddar
  cheese, packed
2 tablespoons sesame
  seeds

½ teaspoon salt
½ teaspoon baking soda
½ cup sour cream

PÂTÉS

A baked pâté, composed of ground meat and other ingredients, may seem to belong to the province of high culinary art, but it is really a glorified meat loaf. And although sometimes more elaborate than a meat loaf, it is not difficult to make. Any butcher will grind the meats for you to your own specifications and you simply assemble and bake.

Pâtés can be baked in earthenware terrines especially designed for the purpose or in a loaf pan. But be sure to select one of pure aluminum or ovenproof pottery or glass. The meat will undergo a chemical reaction if allowed to stand in an alloyed metal or nonenameled iron pan.

The baking dish or pastry crust is always lined with slices of pork fat or blanched bacon. This moistens the pâté as it is baking and, if it is encased in pastry, prevents the crust from cracking. Unless it is en croûte (in pastry), the pâté is then covered and set in a large pan of boiling water, 1½ to 2 inches deep, and put in the oven to bake. Check the water level as it is baking and replenish as needed. If the pâté is to be weighted after baking, empty the pan of water and set it under the terrine to catch any juices which overflow. To weight, use the heaviest object you have that will fit inside the rim of the mold, directly on top of the foil-covered pâté. If you don't happen to have a couple of spare bricks, a 1-quart jar filled with water will do nicely. Leave the weight on the pâté until it has cooled thoroughly.

If you are baking a pâté en croûte, it is best to use a hinged aluminum mold, from which the pâté can easily be released. If you use an ordinary baking dish or loaf pan, make sure it has straight sides and no lip or extension at the upper inside edge which might catch the pâté and prevent it from unmolding. To line the mold with pastry, roll out the dough on a floured board to a thickness of ⅛ inch. Press the mold onto the surface of the dough to make an outline of the bottom of the dish. Remove the mold, cut out the bottom piece, and fit it into your terrine (or place it on top of a baking sheet if you are using a hinged mold without a top and bottom). Then cut a strip of dough as long as the circumference of the mold and 1 inch wider than the height of the mold. Fit it inside, moistening and sealing the seams at the bottom edge. Allow 1 inch to overhang at the top edge. After the pastry casing is lined with fat and filled with pâté, cut another piece of dough for the top crust in the same manner as you cut out the bottom. Fold the 1-inch overhang from the sides onto the top and seal. Cut air vents into the top crust and brush the crust and any decorative pastry cutouts with an egg wash. The pâté is now ready for the oven.

Any of the pâtés in this chapter may be baked in a pastry casing, and conversely, any of those designated en croûte may be baked without a crust. Those which are not en croûte are usually weighted. (Exceptions are the Chicken Liver Pâté, Summer Terrine, and Spinach-Artichoke Pâté which should be light in texture and therefore are not weighted.)

Any of the pâtés may be covered with an aspic, or not, as you will. But pâté gifts which are not en croûte must be left in the baking dish if surrounded with aspic. To cover with aspic, unmold the pâté and remove the layer of fat. Wash and dry the baking dish, and replace the pâté. Stir the aspic over a pan filled with ice cubes until it thickens and is on the verge of setting; then pour it over the pâté. If you like, place decorations such as pimento, herb leaves, lemon slices, hard-cooked egg cutouts, etc., into the aspic before it sets. Refrigerate until firm.

Most pâtés keep well for a week, but the flavor is at its best 2 days after baking. We do not advise freezing pâtés.

✄ PÂTÉ PASTRY

2⅔ cups flour
½ teaspoon salt
¼ pound cold unsalted
 butter, cut up
¼ cup vegetable
 shortening, chilled

2 egg yolks
¼ to ⅓ cup dry white
 wine, well chilled

Combine the flour and salt in a mixing bowl. Cut in the butter and shortening with the tips of your fingers or a pastry blender.

Add the egg yolks and just enough wine to hold the mixture together. Knead the dough for a few turns, form into a ball, cover, and chill well before rolling out.

YIELD: ENOUGH TO LINE A 2-QUART MOLD

❌ ASPIC FOR PÂTÉS

1 envelope unflavored gelatin
1½ cups water
3 tablespoons dry white wine or dry vermouth
2 chicken or beef bouillon cubes

Soften the gelatin in ¼ cup of the water. Pour the remaining water and the wine into a saucepan. Add the bouillon cubes and stir in the softened gelatin. Heat gently, stirring, until very hot and the gelatin is dissolved. Do not boil.

Stir the aspic over a pan filled with ice cubes until it thickens and is about to set before pouring over the pâté.

YIELD: 1 ¾ CUPS ASPIC

❌ CHICKEN LIVER PÂTÉ EN CROÛTE

This is a delicately flavored, light pâté. You may bake it without the pastry casing by placing it in a fat-lined terrine and setting it in a pan of boiling water to bake. Even without the pastry crust, this pâté should not be weighted.

1 pound chicken livers
½ chicken breast,
* skinned and boned*
4 tablespoons unsalted
* butter*
1 cup minced mushrooms
4 scallions, chopped
* (½ cup)*
3 eggs, beaten
¾ cup heavy cream
⅓ cup dry white wine
1 tablespoon cognac
¼ cup flour
½ teaspoon salt
Fresh-ground black
* pepper, to taste*

Pinch of tarragon
Dough for pastry casing
* (page 199)*
¾ pound thin-sliced
* pork fat*
2 whole, skinned and
* boned chicken breasts,*
* marinated for at least*
* 1 hour in ½ cup dry*
* white wine and cut*
* into lengthwise strips*
* ¼ inch thick and*
* ½ inch wide*

FOR EGG WASH
1 egg beaten with 1 tablespoon water

Aspic (page 200)

Purée the chicken livers, the ½ chicken breast, and the butter in a food processor or blender. Place the minced mushrooms in a linen towel and wring out as much moisture as possible. In a mixing bowl, combine the liver purée with the mushrooms, chopped scallions, beaten eggs, heavy cream, wine, cognac, flour, and seasonings. Sauté a spoonful of the mixture and taste for seasoning.

Preheat oven to 350°.

Roll out the pastry dough to ⅛-inch thickness, and line a

2-quart terrine, loaf pan, or hinged pâté en croûte mold, as directed in the introduction to this chapter. Line the inside of the pastry shell along the sides and bottom with pork fat, reserving several strips to cover the top. Spoon in one third of the pâté mixture. Cover with strips of marinated chicken breast, laid lengthwise. Proceed with alternate layers of pâté and chicken breast, ending with a layer of the pâté. Cover with reserved slices of pork fat. Place the top layer of pastry over the mold, sealing around the edges. Brush with egg wash. Decorate with pastry designs cut from scraps of dough and brush them with egg wash. Make incisions in the top crust to allow steam to escape. Place a baking sheet underneath to catch drippings. Bake for approximately 1 hour and 45 minutes. Pâté is done when the juices bubbling up through the crust are clear. Cool on a rack, chill in the refrigerator, and prepare aspic.

Stir the aspic over a pan filled with ice cubes until it thickens and is on the verge of setting. Spoon as much as possible through a vent in the top crust of the chilled pâté. Return the pâté to the refrigerator and chill for 1 hour, or until the aspic is set. Spoon in the rest of the aspic and chill for several hours before unmolding.

YIELD: ONE PÂTÉ

✖ DUCK PÂTÉ EN CROÛTE

This pâté combines duck with several piquant condiments, such as pickles, green olives, and capers, for an unusual effect. To bake it without the pastry casing, fill a fat-lined terrine with the pâté, and bake and weight it according to the instructions in the introduction to this chapter.

One 4½- to 5-pound
duck

FOR THE MARINADE

¼ cup dry white wine
2 tablespoons brandy
¼ teaspoon dried
*   rosemary*
Large pinch savory
1 bay leaf

1 tablespoon chopped
*   fresh parsley*
4 to 5 scallions, chopped
1 clove garlic, peeled
*   and crushed*
1 teaspoon green
*   peppercorns, crushed*

1 large whole chicken
*   breast, skinned and*
*   boned*
¼ pound chicken livers
6 tablespoons unsalted
*   butter, softened*
2 eggs
12 small green pitted
*   olives*
2 tablespoons capers

½ teaspoon salt
Dough for pastry casing
*   (page 199)*
¾ pound thin-sliced
*   pork fat for larding*
4 to 6 sweet midget
*   pickles or cornichons,*
*   halved or quartered*
*   lengthwise*

FOR EGG WASH

1 egg beaten with 1 teaspoon water

Aspic (page 200)

With a small, sharp knife, cut through the skin and fatty layer down the back of the duck. Remove the skin from the entire body (it will pull off easily). Cut the breast meat from the bones in two large pieces. Scrape and cut all the remaining meat from the carcass, legs, and wings. Reserve the liver.

Place the two large pieces of breast meat from the duck in a shallow, wide-bottomed bowl. Combine the marinade ingredients, pour over duck breasts, and marinate for several hours at room temperature, or overnight in the refrigerator.

Grind the remaining duck meat and the chicken breast. Purée the reserved duck liver and the chicken livers with the butter and eggs, and combine with the ground duck and chicken. Stir in the olives, capers, and salt. Remove the duck breasts from the marinade and stir the marinating liquid into the pâté mixture. Sauté a spoonful of the mixture and taste for seasoning. Cut each half duck breast into 4 or 5 lengthwise strips.

Preheat oven to 350°.

Roll out the pastry dough to a thickness of ⅛ inch and line a 1½-quart terrine, loaf pan, or pâté en croûte mold with the dough, reserving a piece for the top. Then line the inside of the pastry shell, along the sides and bottom, with slices of pork fat. Spoon one third of the pâté mixture into the mold. Cover with half of the strips of duck breast and half of the pickles, all laid lengthwise. Add another third of the pâté mixture, cover with remaining strips of duck breast and pickles, and finally, spoon the remaining third of the pâté on top. Cover with slices of pork fat. Roll out pastry to fit the top of the mold; place it over the mold, sealing well with the sides of the pastry casing. Brush with the egg wash and decorate with pastry cutouts. Make incisions in the top crust to allow steam to escape. Place a baking sheet underneath to catch drippings and bake, uncovered, for 2 hours, or until the juices are a clear yellow and a meat thermometer registers about 175°.

Cool on a wire rack; then chill thoroughly in the refrigerator.

Stir the aspic over a pan filled with ice cubes until it thickens and just begins to set. Spoon as much as possible through a vent in the top crust of the chilled pâté. Return the pâté to the refrigerator and chill for 1 hour, or until the aspic is set. Spoon in the rest of the aspic and chill for several hours before unmolding.

YIELD: ONE PÂTÉ

✂ MOCK GAME PÂTÉ

An unusual pâté made with lamb. The ingredients for the marinade, which are those often used in cooking game, give the pâté a game flavor.

FOR THE MARINADE
¼ cup red wine
2 tablespoons brandy
4 crushed juniper
   berries
2 teaspoons crushed
   green peppercorns

1 clove garlic, crushed
1 teaspoon sugar
1 bay leaf
Pinch thyme
Pinch ground cloves
Pinch ground nutmeg

1 large chicken breast,
   skinned and boned
   (about ¾ pound)
½ pound chicken livers
½ cup dried mushrooms
2 eggs
4 tablespoons unsalted
   butter

1 pound ground lamb
   shoulder
4 scallions or shallots,
   chopped
1 teaspoon salt
¾ to 1 pound thin-
   sliced pork fat for
   larding

Combine the ingredients for the marinade and place in a shallow, nonmetallic bowl with the chicken breast and chicken livers. Marinate in the refrigerator several hours or overnight.

Wash the dried mushrooms very well. Put them in a saucepan with more than enough water to cover and simmer gently until they are thoroughly rehydrated. Drain and reserve.

Preheat oven to 325°.

Remove the chicken breast and livers from the marinade, reserving the marinade. Cut half of the breast into 6 long strips and chop the other half fine. Purée the chicken livers in a blender or food processor with the eggs and butter. In a mixing bowl, combine the puréed liver mixture with the finely chopped half chicken breast, the reserved marinade (discarding the bay leaf), the reserved mushrooms, ground lamb, chopped scallions or shallots, and salt.

Line a 1½-quart terrine or baking dish with the pork fat. Ladle in one third of the pâté mixture. Place 3 strips of chicken breast lengthwise over the pâté. Add another layer of pâté, another layer of chicken strips, and a final layer of pâté. Cover with the remaining strips of larding fat. Cover tightly with aluminum foil and lid, if available. Place in a pan of boiling water (1½ to 2 inches deep) and bake in the preheated oven for about 2 hours. Pâté is done when it shrinks from the sides of the pan and the juices run clear. Empty the pan of water, and replace the terrine in the pan on a counter top. Place a heavy object directly on top of the foil-covered pâté and let it stand until cool.

YIELD: ONE PÂTÉ

✂ PÂTÉ DE CAMPAGNE

A traditional pâté de campagne, when cut, reveals identifiable bits of white fat, contributing to a marbleized texture. But to some people, this is not always desirable. The following tastes and looks like an authentic French pâté, with chopped nuts and ham creating a pattern. Should you desire a more distinctly fat-speckled pâté, have your butcher grind 6 to 8 ounces of pork fat with the pork shoulder.

½ pound chicken livers
2 eggs
⅓ cup heavy cream
⅓ cup cognac
½ pound ground veal
    shoulder
½ pound ground pork
    shoulder
6 to 8 ounces ground
    pork fat, optional
1 cup coarse-chopped
    walnuts or pistachio
    nuts

1 clove garlic, peeled
    and crushed
½ teaspoon salt
Fresh-ground black
    pepper, to taste
Pinch of thyme
¼-inch-thick center
    slice of ham
¾ pound thin-sliced
    pork fat for larding

Preheat oven to 350°

Purée the chicken livers in a blender or food processor with the eggs, cream, and cognac. Turn the mixture into a large bowl and combine with all remaining ingredients, except the ham and larding fat, mixing well. Sauté a spoonful of the pâté to taste for seasoning. Slice the ham lengthwise into ½-inch-wide strips.

Line a 1½-quart terrine or loaf pan with the pork fat, reserving

enough to cover the top. Spoon in one third of the pâté. Place half
the ham strips on top. Add another layer of pâté, then the remaining ham strips, and finally the rest of the pâté. Cover with the
reserved pork fat. Cover tightly with aluminum foil and a lid, if
available. Place in a pan of boiling water (1½ to 2 inches deep),
and bake for about 2 hours. The pâté is done when it shrinks
from the sides of the pan and the juices are a clear yellow. A
meat thermometer should register about 170°. Empty the pan
of water, and replace the terrine in the pan on a counter top.
Weight it with a heavy object, placed directly on top of the foil-
covered pâté, until it has cooled.

YIELD: ONE PÂTÉ

℣ SPINACH ARTICHOKE PÂTÉ

This is a meatless pâté delicately flavored with anchovy. It may
be served as a side dish or for luncheon or brunch.

*Three 10-ounce
  packages fresh
  spinach
2 heads Boston lettuce
¼ cup fresh parsley
  sprigs, packed
One 2-ounce can
  anchovy fillets (11
  fillets)
4 eggs
½ cup heavy cream
1 tablespoon fresh
  lemon juice*

*2 tablespoons flour
½ teaspoon nutmeg
Salt and fresh-ground
  black pepper
½ cup water chestnuts,
  quartered
10 medium-sized pitted
  black olives
5 to 6 artichoke hearts,
  cooked, cut in half,
  and well drained
½ pound bacon for
  larding*

Wash the spinach, removing the stems and any wilted leaves. Wash the lettuce and discard the tough outer leaves. Blanch the spinach and lettuce by immersing in a very large pot of boiling water for 2 minutes, or just until wilted. Drain in a colander and press out as much water as possible, using the back of a wooden spoon and squeezing between your hands.

Preheat oven to 375°.

Purée the spinach and lettuce in a food processor or a blender, a little at a time, with the parsley and the anchovy fillets. In a large mixing bowl, beat the eggs; add the cream, lemon juice, puréed spinach mixture, flour, nutmeg, and seasoning to taste, combining all the ingredients well. Stir in the quartered water chestnuts.

Line the bottom and sides of a nonmetallic 1½-quart loaf pan or terrine with strips of bacon. Spoon in half the pâté mixture. Arrange the olives in a row down the center of the pâté and place rows of halved artichoke hearts on either side. Cover with the remainder of the pâté. Cover the top with strips of bacon and place a double thickness of aluminum foil over the top of the pan. Set within a larger baking dish and pour in 1 to 2 inches of boiling water. Bake for 1 hour and 35 minutes to 1 hour and 45 minutes, or until a skewer inserted in the center of the pâté comes out clean. Do not weight this pâté. It may be served warm or at room temperature.

To reheat before serving, cover the pan with aluminum foil and heat for 15 to 20 minutes at 375°.

YIELD: ONE PÂTÉ

❊ SUMMER TERRINE

This is a fragrant terrine, filled with summer herbs, that keeps well in the refrigerator for several days. It is good cold or at room temperature.

¼ *pound bacon*
¾ *pound boned and skinned chicken (1 small breast and thigh)*
¾ *pound boneless veal*
5 *tablespoons unsalted butter*
1 *small onion, chopped fine*
1 *clove garlic, peeled and minced*
2 *tablespoons shallots, peeled and chopped fine*
1 *cup firm-packed chopped parsley*
3 *tablespoons cognac*

1 *egg, lightly beaten*
2 *tablespoons chopped fresh basil, or ¾ teaspoon dried*
2 *tablespoons chopped fresh sage, or ¾ teaspoon dried*
1 *tablespoon fresh tarragon leaves, or ½ teaspoon dried*
1 *teaspoon salt*
½ *teaspoon fresh-ground pepper*
¼ *pound baked ham, cut into strips ¼ inch thick*
4 *sprigs fresh thyme, or ½ teaspoon dried*

Preheat oven to 350°.

Blanch the bacon in boiling water for 3 minutes. Drain well on paper toweling.

Grind together the chicken, veal, and 4 tablespoons butter in a meat grinder or food processor.

Melt the remaining tablespoon of butter in a small skillet and sauté the onion, garlic, and shallots until soft. Stir in ¼ cup of the parsley and sauté 1 minute more. Remove from the heat.

Place the meat mixture and the onion mixture in a large bowl with the cognac, egg, basil, sage, tarragon, salt, and pepper. Mix with your hands until well blended.

Line an 8½-by4½-inch loaf pan with the blanched bacon strips so that they hang over the sides. Place one third of the meat mixture in the pan. Arrange 3 strips of ham lengthwise on top and press down. Press in one third more of the meat mixture and arrange 3 more strips of ham on top. Cover with the remaining meat mixture. Place the fresh thyme sprigs on top, or sprinkle with the dried thyme. Wrap the ends of the bacon around the entire mixture, pressing down gently. Cover tightly with aluminum foil. Place in a baking pan filled with 2 inches of water. Bake for 1 hour, or until the juices run clear.

Remove the aluminum foil and cool the terrine in the pan. Do not weight. Unmold and pour or scrape off any unnecessary fat. Cover and refrigerate until needed. Serve in thin slices.

YIELD: ONE PÂTÉ

SAVORY TARTS & PIES

Y O U will find instructions for making, rolling, and prebaking pastry in the introduction to the chapter on Sweet Tarts and Pies. For all the recipes in this chapter, partially bake the pie shell and brush it with egg white before filling. All the recipes in this chapter should be baked in pie rather than tart pans.

When baking a pie for a gift, cool it thoroughly on a wire rack before wrapping or covering it. Instruct the recipient to reheat it by placing it in the middle of a 350° oven for 15 to 20 minutes, or until it is heated through. If the crust browns too much, cover it loosely with foil.

Many tarts, pies, or quiches may be frozen, but they suffer a loss of quality in the process, and we do not consider them suitable for gift giving. If you do freeze one for home use, let it thaw completely on a wire rack before reheating. Reheat it on the lowest shelf of your oven, at 350°, for 15 to 20 minutes. We find this results in a crisper bottom crust than when reheating directly from the freezer.

Any of the recipes in this chapter may be doubled.

✖ PASTRY CRUST FOR SAVORY TARTS AND PIES

1⅓ cups flour
¼ teaspoon salt
5 tablespoons cold, unsalted butter, cut into small pieces
2 tablespoons cold vegetable shortening
2 to 3 tablespoons ice-cold dry white wine

Combine the flour and salt in a mixing bowl. Cut in the butter and shortening with the tips of your fingers or a pastry blender. Add just enough cold wine to hold the mixture together and form a dough. Knead for a few turns, form into a ball, cover, and chill well before rolling out.

YIELD: ENOUGH FOR THE BOTTOM
CRUST OF A 9-INCH PIE
See also Cheese Crust, page 226.

❧ ARTICHOKE SHRIMP QUICHE

1¼ cups cooked,
  medium-sized shrimp
3 tablespoons chopped
  scallions
1 large clove garlic,
  peeled and crushed
2 tablespoons unsalted
  butter
2 tablespoons dry white
  wine
3 eggs

1 cup buttermilk
½ cup grated Jarlsberg
  cheese, packed
Few drops Tabasco sauce
Salt
4 to 6 artichoke hearts, cut
  into quarters or eighths,
  depending on their size
1 partially baked 9-inch
  pie crust, page 213

Preheat oven to 375°.

Sauté the shrimp, scallions, and garlic with the butter very briefly. Add the wine, turn up the heat, and cook just until the liquid evaporates. Beat the eggs lightly in a mixing bowl. Stir in the buttermilk and the grated cheese. Season to taste with a few drops Tabasco sauce and a little salt. Distribute the sautéed shrimp mixture, and the cut artichoke hearts over the bottom of the pie shell. Pour the custard on top and bake for about 40 minutes, or until a knife inserted in the center comes out clean. Cool on a wire rack.

YIELD: ONE 9-INCH QUICHE

❧ ASPARAGUS QUICHE

This is a variation of a quiche Lorraine, to make in early spring when the first asparagus are in the markets.

You may follow this recipe to make a quiche Lorraine by substituting 4 to 5 slices of crisp, crumbled bacon for the asparagus and adding a tablespoon of minced onion.

3 eggs
1¼ cups light cream or
half-and-half
¾ cup grated Jarlsberg
cheese or good, full-
flavored Swiss, packed
6 tablespoons fresh-grated
Parmesan cheese
12 cooked asparagus
spears, trimmed and cut
into 1-inch lengths

1 tablespoon chopped
fresh parsley
Fresh-ground black
pepper
1 partially baked 9-inch
pie crust, page 213

Preheat oven to 375°.

Beat the eggs lightly and stir in the cream or half-and-half, the grated Jarlsberg or Swiss cheese, and 3 tablespoons of the grated Parmesan cheese. Fold in the asparagus pieces and the chopped parsley, and season to taste with fresh-ground black pepper. Ladle into the prepared pie shell. Sprinkle the remaining Parmesan over the top. Bake for 45 minutes, or until a knife inserted in the center comes out clean. Cool on a wire rack.

YIELD: ONE 9-INCH QUICHE

❈ CRABMEAT QUICHE

3 eggs, lightly beaten
1 cup plus 1 tablespoon
  buttermilk or light
  cream
4 ounces Jarlsberg cheese,
  grated (1 cup, packed)
  or use a flavorful Swiss
  cheese
6 tablespoons fresh-grated
  Parmesan cheese

1 tablespoon dry sherry
½ small yellow onion,
  minced
3 to 6 ounces cooked fresh
  crabmeat, or frozen
  crabmeat, thawed and
  drained
1 partially baked 9-inch
  pie crust, page 213

Preheat oven to 375°.

Combine the beaten eggs, buttermilk, grated Jarlsberg cheese, 4 tablespoons (¼ cup) of the grated Parmesan cheese, and the sherry. Distribute the onion and crabmeat over the bottom of the prepared pie crust. Spoon in the custard mixture. Sprinkle the reserved Parmesan over the top. Bake for 35 to 40 minutes, or until a knife inserted in the center comes out clean.

YIELD: ONE 9-INCH QUICHE

❈ LEEK STILTON QUICHE

Stilton has a unique flavor; don't substitute any other cheese if it is unavailable.

3 *medium-sized leeks*
2 *tablespoons chopped*
  shallots
2 *tablespoons unsalted*
  butter
3 *eggs, lightly beaten*
1½ *cups half-and-half*
4 *ounces Stilton cheese,*
  crumbled

¼ *teaspoon fresh-ground*
  nutmeg
⅛ *teaspoon fresh-ground*
  pepper, or to taste
⅛ *teaspoon salt, or to*
  taste
1 *partially baked 9-inch*
  pie crust, page 213

Preheat oven to 375°.

Wash the leeks carefully, being certain to wash out all the grit between the fronds. Cut off the upper third of the leaves and discard. Chop the remaining two thirds of the leeks. Sauté the leeks and the shallots in the butter until soft.

Stir the eggs into the half-and-half. Add the leek mixture, then the crumbled Stilton. Add the nutmeg and pepper and taste for seasoning. Add the salt, if necessary. Pour into the partially baked pie crust.

Bake for 40 to 45 minutes, or until a knife inserted in the center of the custard comes out clean.

YIELD: ONE 9-INCH QUICHE

❧ MEDITERRANEAN TART

This is a hearty and colorful dish—brimming with vegetables, ham, and cheese, and garnished with tomato wedges and parsley. It would be especially welcome on a brisk fall or winter day.

1 *small sweet green pepper, seeded and sliced in ¼-inch strips*
1½ *tablespoons olive oil*
2 *large cloves garlic, peeled and crushed*
1 *medium yellow onion, sliced*
1 *tablespoon flour*
2 *eggs*
1 *cup sour cream*
⅔ *cup grated Jarlsberg cheese, packed, or flavorful Swiss cheese*
Fresh-ground black pepper

One 4-ounce-slice *baked ham, cut into strips (about ⅔ cup)*
½ *cup pitted black olives, cut in halves*
1 *partially baked 9-inch pie crust, page 213*
2 *to 3 tablespoons fresh-grated Parmesan cheese*
1 *medium-sized ripe tomato, seeded and sliced into 8 wedges*
1 *tablespoon chopped fresh parsley, packed*

Preheat oven to 375°.

Sauté the green pepper strips in the olive oil for 10 minutes. Add the garlic and onion to the skillet and sauté for 10 to 15 minutes longer, or until the vegetables are tender but not brown. Stir in the flour. In a mixing bowl, beat the eggs lightly and stir in the sour cream and the grated Jarlsberg or Swiss cheese. Add fresh-ground black pepper to taste. Distribute the sautéed vegetables, the ham strips, and the halved black olives evenly over the bottom of the prepared pie shell. Pour the custard over this and sprinkle the surface with the grated Parmesan cheese. Bake for 30 minutes. Then arrange the seeded tomato wedges in a circular pattern around the quiche and sprinkle with the chopped parsley. Return to the oven and continue baking 15 minutes longer, or until a knife inserted in the center comes out clean. Cool on a wire rack.

YIELD: ONE 9-INCH TART

✖ MUSHROOM TART

The sautéed mushrooms in this quiche are subtly flavored with lemon juice and dry white wine. We have omitted any grated cheese from this recipe, as we feel it obscures the delicate flavor of the mushrooms.

1½ pounds firm white mushrooms
6 scallions (white part only) or shallots, chopped
3 tablespoons unsalted butter
⅓ cup dry white wine

2 tablespoons lemon juice
3 eggs
1¼ cups heavy cream
Pinch of nutmeg
Salt and fresh-ground black pepper
1 partially baked 9-inch pie crust, page 213

Rinse the mushrooms briefly under running water or wipe clean with a damp towel. (Do not get them waterlogged.) Dry and slice. Put them into a large skillet with the chopped scallions or shallots and the butter. Sprinkle with wine and lemon juice and sauté gently for a few minutes. Turn up the heat and boil until the liquid has evaporated, stirring to prevent the mushrooms from sticking and scorching. As soon as all the liquid has disappeared from the pan, remove from the heat.

Preheat oven to 375°.

In a mixing bowl, beat the eggs lightly and mix in the cream. Add the mushrooms, a pinch of nutmeg, and a little salt and fresh-ground pepper. Spoon into the prepared pie crust and bake for 40 to 45 minutes, or until a knife inserted in the center comes out clean.

YIELD: ONE 9-INCH TART

SEA QUICHE

This is a delicately flavored quiche made with scallops. It is a nice supper dish, served with dry white wine and a salad of fresh greens.

1 pound scallops	*1 tablespoon chopped*
2 tablespoons lemon	*chives*
juice	*Pinch of salt*
2 tablespoons dry white	*Fresh-ground black*
wine	*pepper*
3 eggs	*1 partially baked 9-inch*
¾ cup heavy cream	*pie crust, page 213*
½ cup sour cream	*1½ tablespoons fresh-*
1 tablespoon chopped	*grated Parmesan cheese*
fresh parsley	

If the scallops are the large ocean variety, cut them into thirds or quarters. Combine the scallops with the lemon juice and white wine and marinate in the refrigerator for several hours in a shallow, flat-bottomed bowl, stirring occasionally.

Preheat oven to 375°.

In a large mixing bowl, beat the eggs lightly. Stir in the heavy

cream, sour cream, chopped parsley, chopped chives, a small
pinch of salt, and fresh-ground black pepper to taste. Drain the
scallops well, and distribute them evenly over the bottom of the
prepared pie shell. Pour the custard mixture on top and sprinkle
with the Parmesan cheese. Bake for 45 minutes, or until a knife
inserted in the center comes out clean. Cool on a wire rack.

YIELD: ONE 9-INCH QUICHE

✖ SMOKED SALMON QUICHE

This is a good main dish for a Sunday brunch. Taste the salmon
before using it. If it is too salty, soak it in ½ cup milk for 30
minutes and drain well.

*¼ cup chopped
  scallions
½ tablespoon unsalted
  butter
2 tablespoons dry white
  wine
3 eggs, lightly beaten
1½ cups sour cream
6 ounces smoked
  salmon, slivered
  (preferably Nova
  Scotia)*

*1½ tablespoons fresh
  dill weed, or 1½
  teaspoons dried
Fresh-ground white
  pepper
1 partially baked 9-inch
  pie crust, page 213*

Preheat oven to 375°.
   Sauté the scallions in the butter and wine over medium-high
heat until the liquid has evaporated. Stir the eggs into the sour

cream. Add the sautéed scallions and the slivered salmon. Stir in the dill and pepper, to taste. Pour into the partially baked crust and bake for 40 to 45 minutes, or until a knife inserted into the center of the custard comes out clean.

YIELD: ONE 9-INCH QUICHE

⚓ SPINACH ROQUEFORT QUICHE

10 ounces fresh
spinach, washed and
stemmed, but not
chopped, or one
10-ounce package
frozen, chopped
spinach
4 ounces (⅔ cup)
mild Roquefort or
blue cheese, crumbled
1⅓ cups sour cream

3 eggs, lightly beaten
5 tablespoons fresh-
grated Parmesan
cheese
½ teaspoon
Worcestershire sauce
1 partially baked 9-inch
pie crust, page 213

Preheat oven to 375°.

Blanch the spinach in a large pot of boiling water for 2 minutes, or until wilted. Drain thoroughly, pressing out as much water as possible. Combine it with the Roquefort or blue cheese, sour cream, beaten eggs, 3 tablespoons Parmesan cheese, and the Worcestershire sauce. Spoon the mixture into the prepared pie crust. Sprinkle the remaining Parmesan over the top and bake for 45 minutes, or until a knife inserted in the center comes out clean.

YIELD: ONE 9-INCH QUICHE

⚜ SPINACH TOMATO PIE

This is a very mild pie, basically a puréed spinach, garnished with tomato slices and bacon. It should be served as a side dish or for a light luncheon. You may use frozen spinach, but the taste of fresh is worth the little extra effort.

*Three 10-ounce packages
fresh spinach, washed
and chopped, or 3
packages frozen
chopped spinach,
partially thawed
1 tablespoon flour
½ cup heavy cream
½ cup sour cream
2 eggs, lightly beaten
1 teaspoon
Worcestershire sauce*

*Nutmeg, salt, and fresh-
ground black pepper
1 partially baked 9-inch
pie crust, page 213
1 medium-sized ripe
tomato, sliced thick and
seeded
5 to 6 slices bacon,
sautéed and crumbled
4 to 5 chopped scallions*

Preheat oven to 375°.

Blanch the spinach in a large pot of boiling water for 2 minutes, or until wilted and drain well. Purée in a blender or food processor. In a mixing bowl, combine the puréed spinach with the flour. Stir in the heavy cream, sour cream, eggs, Worcestershire sauce, and seasonings to taste. Turn into the prepared pie crust. Bake for 25 minutes. Arrange a circle of tomato slices on top. Sprinkle with crumbled bacon and chopped scallions and bake for 15 minutes longer, or until a knife inserted in the center comes out clean. Cover loosely with foil during the latter part of baking if the crust browns too much.

YIELD: ONE 9-INCH PIE

⚛ SUMMER PIE

This is a way to enjoy the bounty of a summer garden. It is light and delicate, suitable for a hot evening or afternoon. By using only 1 egg and a minimum quantity of milk and cheese to bind the squash, the dish has the added advantage of being low in calories.

1 medium-to-large
   yellow squash
⅓ cup milk
⅓ cup fresh-grated
   Parmesan cheese
1 egg, lightly beaten
¼ teaspoon salt or to
   taste
Fresh-ground white
   pepper
2 tablespoons chopped
   fresh basil, or 1
   teaspoon dried

2 tablespoons fresh
   savory leaves, or 1
   teaspoon dried
1 partially baked 9-inch
   pie crust, page 213
1 very large or 2 medium
   ripe tomatoes
1 tablespoon minced fresh
   parsley

Preheat oven to 350°.

Scrub the squash gently with a brush until clean. Don't peel it unless the skin is quite blemished. Grate the squash by hand or in a food processor. Scrape the grated squash into a large bowl; there should be about 1½ to 2 cups. Drain if necessary. Add the milk, cheese, egg, the salt and pepper to taste, basil, and savory and combine well. Pour into the partially baked pie crust and smooth it over. Cut the tomato into slices about ⅓ to ½ inch thick and arrange on top of the squash mixture. Bake for 50 to 60 minutes, or until the custard is set. Cool for 5 minutes. Sprinkle with the parsley and serve. If desired, serve with additional grated cheese.

YIELD: ONE 9-INCH PIE

⟨ TARTE À L'OIGNON

We learned to make a true Alsatian *tarte à l'oignon* from Marion Fulbright, who, with her husband, spent a year in Strasbourg in a region of unique French cuisine. The local *tarte à l'oignon,* a hearty, dense, and aromatic tribute to the onion, was a favorite of the Fulbrights. This tart is not a custardy quiche, but is composed almost entirely of sautéed onions.

6 cups thin-sliced onions (about 2½ pounds)
4 tablespoons butter
1 tablespoon flour
1 egg, lightly beaten
1 cup grated Jarlsberg cheese or a flavorful Swiss cheese, packed (4 ounces)
¼ cup fresh-grated Parmesan cheese

⅓ cup buttermilk or light cream
½ teaspoon Worcestershire sauce
1 partially baked 9-inch pie crust, page 213
4 to 5 slices bacon, diced and parboiled for 2 minutes

Sauté the onions in the butter in a large skillet. Sprinkle with the flour and continue cooking until very soft.

Preheat oven to 375°.

In a mixing bowl, combine the cooked onions, beaten egg, grated cheeses, buttermilk, and Worcestershire sauce. Spoon into the prepared pie crust. Sprinkle diced bacon over the surface. Bake for 45 minutes, or until a knife inserted in the center comes out clean.

YIELD: ONE 9-INCH TART

✕ TORTA RUSTICA

A colorful, aromatic pie which can be refrigerated for several days. It is good to take along on a picnic.

FOR THE CHEESE CRUST
> 2¼ cups sifted flour
> 5 ounces Cheddar cheese, grated
> 3 tablespoons cold vegetable shortening
> 6 tablespoons unsalted butter
> 2 to 4 tablespoons cold white wine

FOR THE FILLING
> 1 medium onion, chopped coarse
> 1 large clove garlic, peeled and minced
> 4 tablespoons unsalted butter
> 12 ounces lean ground beef
> 6 ounces lean ground pork
> 4 eggs
> 2 tablespoons tomato paste
> 1 cup fresh-grated Parmesan cheese
> ½ teaspoon basil

½ cup chopped parsley
½ teaspoon marjoram
Fresh-ground pepper
2 pounds fresh spinach,
    cooked, drained well,
    and chopped, or two
    10-ounce packages

frozen chopped
    spinach, drained well
2 large roasted red
    peppers (page 186), or
    one 8-ounce jar
4 ounces mozzarella
    cheese, shredded

FOR THE GLAZE
1 egg beaten with 1 tablespoon water

TO PREPARE THE CRUST

Put the flour in a large bowl. Add the grated cheese and the cold shortening and butter in small pieces. Cut them in with a pastry cutter until the mixture is crumbly. Add the wine and stir it in lightly. With your hands, combine the dough into a ball. Roll out two thirds of the dough and line a 9-inch pie plate. Refrigerate the remaining one third.

Preheat oven to 350°.

TO PREPARE THE FILLING

Sauté the onion and garlic in 2 tablespoons butter until soft. Add the meats and sauté until no longer pink. Beat 2 eggs lightly and stir into the meat. Stir in the tomato paste, ½ cup Parmesan cheese, and the basil, parsley, marjoram, and pepper to taste. Remove from heat.

Sauté the chopped spinach in the remaining 2 tablespoons butter. Remove from the heat. Beat the remaining 2 eggs lightly and stir them into the spinach. Add the remaining ½ cup Parmesan cheese.

Spread half the meat mixture on top of the pie crust. Press half the spinach on top of the meat. Arrange the peppers on the spinach, then sprinkle on the shredded mozzarella. Spread the remaining spinach over the mozarella, and top with the remaining meat mixture.

Roll out the remaining pastry and place it on top of the filled pie, crimping the edges to seal. Cut slits into the top crust to allow steam to escape. Decorate with pastry cutouts, if desired. Brush with the egg glaze.

Bake for 50 to 60 minutes, or until browned. It can be served warm or at room temperature.

YIELD: ONE 9-INCH PIE

POTPOURRI

THIS chapter includes gifts from your kitchen which are not necessarily edible, such as pomanders and potpourri, as well as spiced teas, coffees, and cider. Any of the recipes may be doubled.

BAKER'S CLAY CHERRY PIE

This is a beautiful, appetizing pie, and you'll never have to bake another, because this one will last forever. Made out of "baker's clay," a hard, salt dough, then baked and varnished, it is an amusing *objet* for a kitchen or informal dining area. The varnish gives it an attractive glaze, and it is remarkably realistic looking. No one would guess that it is not edible. As long as you don't bring it to your next potluck supper, your friends will be delighted with it.

FOR THE DOUGH
>   *4 cups flour*
>   *1½ cups salt*
>   *1⅔ cups water*

FOR PAINTING AND VARNISHING

*Dark red acrylic paint,
thinned with a little
water or poster paint
(or bright red mixed
with a little blue to
produce a cherry
shade)
1 small can clear, glossy
varnish or clear
shellac*

*1 small paintbrush for
coloring cherries
1 brush for varnishing
(1 to 2 inches wide)
Varnish or shellac
cleaner for the brush*

TO MAKE THE DOUGH

Combine the flour and salt in a mixing bowl. Add the water and
mix well with your hands. The dough should be firm, but slightly
moist. Add a few more drops of water if necessary. Knead for a
minute until the dough is smooth. Lightly flour a board and roll
out half the dough into a circle ¼ inch thick. (Keep any dough
you are not working with covered with plastic wrap to prevent
it from drying out.) Lightly grease a 7-inch pie dish and line it
with the circle of dough. Trim and flute the edges. Roll small,
cherry-sized balls between the palms of your hands and pile them
loosely into the pie crust. Paint the cherries with dark red paint,
pushing your brush down between the cherries to paint any that
are visible underneath. In painting the cherries around the outer

edge, be careful not to get paint on the crust. After you are finished painting, scrape off any red spots on the crust with the point of a knife. Place the pie in the oven, set the temperature to 350°, and bake for 15 minutes, or until the paint is dry. Remove from the oven to a wire rack and allow to cool thoroughly.

Meanwhile, roll out the remaining dough into a rectangle ⅛ to 3/16 inch thick and about 9 inches long. Cut 10 strips of dough, each ½ inch wide, for the lattice top. Lay 5 of them, evenly spaced, across the top of the cooled pie. Lay the remaining strips in the opposite direction, weaving across over and under, the warp and the woof interlacing alternately. When all the strips are woven, trim the edges and press them into the fluted edge of the pie crust. Return to the oven and bake for an additional 2 to 2½ hours, until the pie has hardened. (The lattice top may appear to be too pale, but it will take on a realistic golden tint after varnishing.) Remove the pie from its pan, set on a wire rack, and cool thoroughly. Then paint the entire pie, covering all exposed surfaces, with a clear varnish or shellac. (Allow the top to dry before turning over to varnish the sides and bottom.) For a higher gloss, dry overnight and then give it a second coat.

❧ BAKER'S CLAY BREAD BASKET

This is a hard, durable basket with a varnished finish which gives it the appearance of glazed pottery. It is a clever way to package any baked goods, and can be used afterward as a bread basket. It is made by weaving strips of baker's clay in lattice fashion over the outside of an inverted round mold.

1 recipe for baker's clay   *1 brush, 1 to 2 inches*
dough, page 230   *wide*
One *2-inch-deep metal*   *Varnish or shellac*
pie pan for molding   *cleaner for the brush*
Elmer's glue
1 small can clear
varnish or shellac

Make the dough as directed. Roll out half the dough on a lightly floured board (keep the rest covered with plastic wrap) to a thickness of ⅛ to 3/16 inch. Cut long strips ½ inch wide. Invert the mold and grease the outside surface lightly. Place parallel strips of dough over the bottom and two sides of the pan, leaving ⅜-to-½-inch space between the strips. Weave in the crosswise strips, over and under in a basket-weave pattern. Make 2 more extra-long strips of dough and weave them in and out around the sides of the pan. Work quickly so that the dough does not dry out, and if you are interrupted, cover the lattice with a wet towel. After the weaving is completed, trim the ends of the strips. Break off another piece of dough and, rolling it against the board with the palms of your hands, make a rope ⅜ inch in diameter and as long as the circumference of the rim of the mold. Slip it under the edges of the lattice strips. Moisten the ends of the strips and press them against the rope to seal. Smooth any rough surfaces with the blade of a knife. Place the inverted mold on top of a cookie sheet, set the oven at 300°, and bake for 1½ hours, or until the dough is hard and dry. After it has baked, loosen the edges of the mold with the point of a knife and lift it out. Cool the basket on a wire rack.

Make a decorative edge for the top of the basket by rolling another rope, ½ inch thick. Squeeze a strip of Elmer's glue over the top edge of the basket and lay the rope on top. Press a skewer or narrow stick diagonally into the rope at 1½-inch intervals to make ridges. Cover the basket, inside and out, with aluminum foil to prevent further browning, leaving the rope edge exposed. Return the basket to the oven (right side up) and bake for 30 minutes, or until the rope is hardened and browned. Cool thoroughly. Varnish or shellac all exposed surfaces, inside and out, allowing one side to dry before coating the other. Dry overnight and varnish a second time for a higher gloss finish.

✖ MULLED CIDER MIX

This turns apple cider into a warm, spicy treat for a chilly fall afternoon or evening.

3 cinnamon sticks,
broken up
1 tablespoon whole
allspice
½ teaspoon ground
cinnamon
1½ teaspoons dried
orange peel

1 teaspoon anise seeds
1 teaspoon whole cloves
1 tablespoon coarse-
chopped dried apple,
optional

Mix all the ingredients together. Package in a small muslin or cheesecloth bag tied together with a string. Attach the following instructions: Place spice packet and 6 to 8 cups good apple cider in a saucepan. Bring to a boil and simmer slowly for 15 minutes. Remove the spice bag. Serve hot with a whole cinnamon stick in each cup. If desired, ½ cup rum can be added to the cider while simmering.

YIELD: ENOUGH MIX FOR TWO QUARTS OF CIDER

✂ ORANGE POMANDER

Pomanders are welcome gifts at any time of year, although in sixteenth-century England it was customary to give an orange stuck with cloves as a New Year's gift. Hung in a closet or left in a chest of drawers, they will impart a spicy scent to clothing and linens for many months.

Select firm, unbruised, thin-skinned oranges. We suggest using small ones, since they can be completed more quickly; and there is no reason why you can't make a pomander out of a lemon or an apple, if you prefer.

For 1 small orange, you will need 1 box (1⅛ ounces) whole cloves, a sharp metal skewer, and ground spices, as described below.

Pierce the skin of the orange with the skewer and insert a clove. Repeat, studding the entire surface, except for a small space at the top and bottom through which a ribbon may be threaded. The cloves should be set close together, but not too close, as there is a danger of tearing the skin of the orange. Set them in carefully, always piercing the skin first with the skewer. When the orange has been covered with cloves, mix in a small bowl any or all of the following spices, to total 2 to 3 teaspoons: cinnamon, nutmeg, allspice, mace, ground cloves. Sprinkle the pomander with the spice mixture, covering all the orange skin visible between the cloves. With a long, large-eyed needle, thread a piece of string through the pomander, top to bottom. Leave it uncovered in a cool, dry place to dry out. This will take 2 or 3 weeks; do not be alarmed if it develops a moldy odor during this time. The odor will disappear when the orange is completely dry. After it has dried out, tie a decorative ribbon, about ½ yard long, to the top end of the string and pull it through the orange. Discard the string and knot the ribbon at the bottom of the pomander to secure it. Make a loop with the length of ribbon remaining at the top of the pomander, so that it can be hung.

Potpourri

Infinite varieties of blends are possible, and you may, of course, substitute and experiment as you wish. Package in small apothecary jars to give as potpourri, or enclose in sachets made as follows: with pinking shears, cut 1 square of lightweight patterned fabric and 1 square of organdy or dotted Swiss. Sew together by topstitching around three sides, ½ inch from the edge. Fill loosely with potpourri and topstitch the remaining seam.

Mix together the ingredients of any of the following combinations:

❌ OLD ROSE POTPOURRI

1 cup dried rosebuds
½ cup dried marigolds
¾ cup dried orange peel
½ cup dried hibiscus
4 tablespoons whole
   cloves, several
   crushed

6 cinnamon sticks,
   broken up
1 vanilla bean, cut into
   ¼-inch pieces
8 drops oil of rose
4 drops oil of lemon or
   orange

❌ SUMMER MEADOW POTPOURRI

1 cup dried clover
1 cup dried lavender
¼ cup persimmon bark,
   optional
½ cup dried violets
1 tablespoon dried
   crushed bay leaves

1 tablespoon dried
   rosemary
1 tablespoon dried (not
   powdered) crushed
   sage leaves
6 drops oil of violet

❌ PINE FOREST POTPOURRI

1 cup cedar needles, or
   any soft evergreen
¼ cup persimmon bark
¼ cup dried orange
   peel

2 tablespoons, or a
   small handful
   immature green pine
   cones, if available
3 tablespoons anise seed
6 drops pine or cedar oil

Note: Many potpourri ingredients can be purchased in specialty food stores or in the spice departments of supermarkets. Others can be found in stores which sell ingredients for natural or herbal teas and cosmetic preparations.

Spiced Coffees

We think that these coffees taste best with cream and sugar. They are good enough to double as dessert. Be certain that each gift is labeled and accompanied by the proper instructions.

ALMOND COFFEE

1 cup ground coffee, not instant
½ cup coarse-ground almonds
1 whole vanilla bean, minced
1 teaspoon fresh-ground nutmeg
⅛ teaspoon almond extract

Combine all ingredients. Instruct the recipient to use the coffee in any drip or filter coffee maker, at 1½ times the normal strength, and to use within 2 weeks.
YIELD: APPROXIMATELY SIXTEEN CUPS BREWED COFFEE

❧ MOCHA COFFEE

> *1 cup ground coffee, not instant*
> *½ cup unsweetened cocoa*
> *4 cinnamon sticks, broken into tiny pieces*

Combine all ingredients. Instruct the recipient to use the coffee in any drip or filter coffee maker at double the normal strength. YIELD: APPROXIMATELY TWELVE CUPS BREWED COFFEE

❧ ORANGE OR LEMON COFFEE

> *1 cup ground coffee, not instant*
> *6 tablespoons dried orange or lemon peel*
> *2 teaspoons fresh-ground nutmeg*
> *½ teaspoon ground cardamom*

Combine all ingredients. Instruct the recipient to use the coffee in any drip or filter coffee maker, at 1½ times the normal strength. YIELD: APPROXIMATELY SIXTEEN CUPS BREWED COFFEE

Spiced Teas

These are a refreshing change from plain tea, and any tea drinker would be pleased to receive them as a gift. You may use any type of tea, but unless you are certain of the recipient's tastes, use a high quality, somewhat mild black tea. The teas should be presented loose, in an attractive container. Include a label and the following directions: Use 1 heaping teaspoon for each cup of tea, plus 1 teaspoon for the pot.

The following proportions yield approximately 1 cup, and may, of course, be increased as you like:

✖ ORANGE SPICE TEA

½ cup tea
⅓ cup dried orange peel
2 cinnamon sticks, broken up
2 teaspoons whole cloves

✖ LEMON MINT TEA

¾ cup tea (particularly good made with green tea)
¼ cup dried lemon balm or dried lemon verbena
⅓ cup dried peppermint or spearmint leaves

❧ SPICED TEA

¾ cup tea
2 tablespoons anise seeds
1 tablespoon whole coriander
1 tablespoon whole allspice

❧ ROSE TEA

½ cup tea (best made with a very mild tea)
¼ cup rose hips, crushed after measuring
¼ cup dried rosebuds
¼ cup dried hibiscus
One 2-inch-piece vanilla bean, minced

Index

Almond(s): apple almond tart, 104; choco-
late almond thins, 71; coffee, 237; Mrs.
Beeton's almond cake, 53; paste, 11, 49,
104, 133; spiced, 190; strawberry
almond tart, 121
Apple: -almond tart, 104; -mint chutney,
164; -oatmeal bread, 15
Apricot: conserve, 158; -custard tart, 114;
-filled cookies, 95; -honey bread, 16
Artichoke: -shrimp quiche, 214; spinach
artichoke pâté, 208
Asparagus quiche, 214
Aspic, for pâtés, 200
Aunt Mamie's fruit cake, 61

Basil vinegar, 171
Baker's clay: bread basket, 231; cherry pie,
229; dough for, 230
Banana chocolate tart, 116
Beet conserve, 159
Blueberry: jam, 154; tea cake, 17
Brandied peaches, 152
Brandy, note on use of, 11
Breads, quick: apple oatmeal bread, 15;
apricot honey bread, 16; blueberry tea
cake, 17; Christmas tea cake, 18; Irish
soda bread, 19; lime tea cake, 20; orange
tea cake, 21; pumpkin cider bread, 22;
Vermont whole wheat bread, 23;
zucchini bread, 24

Breads, yeast: cheese, 28; cottage rye, 29;
country wheat, 30; dill, 32; Hunter's, 33;
Mediterranean, 34; Morccan, 36; pub
loaf, 37; sour cream chive, 38
Bread basket, baker's clay, 231
Brownies, Gertrud Blue's, 80
Butter, note on use of, 11
Butters, flavored: caper, 181; green
peppercorn, 180; lemon dill, 179;
mustard shallot, 180; shrimp, 187;
Stilton, 189
Butter cream, chocolate, 56
Butterscotch sauce, 139

Cakes: Aunt Mamie's fruit cake, 61;
chestnut torte, 42; chocolate Chantilly
cake, 43; chocolate valentine cake, 47;
dark Christmas cake, 69; light fruit cake,
62; Mother's Day cake, 49; Mrs.
Beeton's almond cake, 53; Mrs. Isabella
Beeton's unrivalled plum pudding, 63;
old-fashioned birthday cake, 54; seed
cake, 55; spiced fruit cake, 66; Tony's
birthday cake, 56; twelfth cake, 58; white
Christmas cake, 68
Cakes, small. See Cookies and Small Cakes
Candies. See Confections
Caper(s): butter, 181; herb and caper
mayonnaise, 174; sauce, 173
Caponata, 182

Caraway seed cake, 55
Cheddar cheese: note on use of, 11; -sesame crackers, 196; thins, 192
Cheese: asparagus quiche, 214; bits, 193; bread, 28; Cheddar sesame crackers, 196; Cheddar thins, 192; herb Parmesan biscuits, 194; leek Stilton quiche, 216; Mediterranean tart, 217; Parmesan, note on use of, 12; pastry crust, 226; pub loaf, 37; quiche Lorraine, 215; spinach Roquefort quiche, 222; Stilton butter, 189; Swiss, note on use of, 11; Swiss thin, 193; tarte à l'oignon, 225
Cherry pie, baker's clay, 229
Chestnut(s): in brandy syrup, 151; torte, 42
Chicken livers: chopped, 183; chopped with mushrooms, 184; pâté en croûte, 200
Chive bread, with sour cream, 38
Chocolate: -almond thins, 71; banana chocolate tart, 116; brownies, Gertrud Blue's, 80; butter cream, 56; Chantilly cake, 43; -coated marzipan, 134; -coated tiles, 72; disks, 128; Easter eggs, 129; fudge, 130; fudge pie, 105; -ginger tassies, 73; leaves, 96; mint wafers, 131; note on use of, 12; orange chocolate tart, 114; pear chocolate tart, 116; -pecan pie, 106; sauce, 140; surprise cakes, 92; truffles, 132; valentine cake, 47; wedding cakes, 75·
Christmas cake: dark, 69; white, 68
Chutney: apple mint, 164; cranberry pear, 165; mango papaya, 165; quince, 167; Seckel pear, 168; tomato, 177
Cider: mulled, mix, 233; pumpkin cider bread, 22
Cinnamon bows, 76
Citrus rind, note on use of, 12
Cocoa: -dusted marzipan, 133; fudge, 130; -mint patties, 136
Coconut, chocolate Easter eggs, 129
Coffee(s): almond, 237; lemon, 238; mocha, 238; orange, 238
Cognac, note on use of, 11
Confections: butterscotch sauce, 139; candied grapefruit peel, 126; candied orange peel, 126; chestnuts in brandy syrup, 151; chocolate disks, 128; chocolate-coated marzipan, 134; chocolate Easter eggs, 129; chocolate fudge, 130; chocolate mint wafers, 131; chocolate sauce, 140; chocolate truffles, 132; cocoa-dusted marzipan, 133; cocoa

mint patties, 136; glazed spiced nuts, 134; hard sauce, 65; maple walnut sauce, 141; mocha fudge, 131; orange walnut sauce, 141; pastel mint patties, 135; pear ginger sauce, 156; rose pecans, 136 sugared pecans, 138; sugarplums, 137
Conserves: apricot, 158; beet, 159; cranberry orange, 160; pear mincemeat, 161; plum, 162
Cookies and Small Cakes: apricot-filled cookies, 95; chocolate almond thins, 71; chocolate-coated tiles, 72; chocolate ginger tassies, 73; chocolate leaves, 96; chocolate wedding cakes, 75; cinnamon bows, 76; dream bars, 77; Florentine nut wafers, 88; fortune cookies, 79; Gertrud Blue's brownies, 80; kifli, 81; lime tea cakes, 82; Linzer cakes, 84; marmalade petits fours, 92; Miss Elizabeth Holahan's fine tea cakes, 85; mocha meringues, 86; nut wafers, 87; orange flower cakes, 88; orange wedding cakes, 89; petits fours, 90; rolled cookies, 94; surprise cakes, 92
Cottage rye bread, 29
Country wheat bread, 30
Crabmeat quiche, 216
Crackers: Cheddar sesame crackers, 196; Cheddar thins, 192; cheese bits, 193; herb Parmesan biscuits, 194; sesame oat crackers, 195; Swiss thins, 193
Cranberry: -orange tea cake (Christmas tea cake), 18; -orange conserve, 160; -pear chutney, 165; pear cranberry tart, 118

Dark Christmas cake, 69
Dill: bread, 32; lemon butter, 179; vinegar, 171
Dream bars, 77
Duck pâté en croûte, 202

Easter eggs, chocolate, 129
Eggs, note on use of, 12

Flaky pie crust, 101
Flavorings, synthetic, note on use of, 13
Florentine nut wafers, 88
Flour, note on use of, 12
Fortune cookies, 79
Fruit cakes: Aunt Mamie's, 61; dark Christmas, 69; light, 62; Mrs. Isabella Beeton's unrivalled plum pudding, 63; spiced, 66; white Christmas, 68
Fudge: chocolate, 130; mocha, 131

Game pâté, mock, 205
Gertrud Blue's brownies, 80
Ginger: chocolate ginger tassies, 73; pear ginger jam, 155; pear ginger sauce, 156
Gift packaging, 7
Grapefruit peel, candied, 126
Green peppercorn butter, 180

Hard sauce, 65
Herb(s): as an ingredient, 12; -caper mayonnaise, 174; Mediterranean herb bread, 34; -Parmesan biscuits, 194; -red wine vinegar, 170; vinegar, 171, 172; -white wine vinegar, 171
Hibiscus, note on use of, 13
Honey: apricot honey bread, 16; country wheat bread, 30; pear ginger jam, 155; pear ginger sauce, 156
Hunter's bread, 33

Icing and Frosting: almond, 49; chocolate, 42, 96; pastel, 47, 49
Irish soda bread, 19

Jams: blueberry, 154; pear ginger, 155; spiced peach, 156; strawberry, 157; see also Preserves
Jellies: rose petal, 147; sage tracklement, 148; sweet violet, 149; true mint, 150

Kentucky sweet potato pie, 109
Kifli, 81
Kiwi strawberry tart, 110
Kneading dough, 26

Lamb. See Mock game pâté
Leek Stilton quiche, 216
Lemon: -dill butter, 179; -flavored coffee, 238; juice, note on use of, 12; -mint tea, 239; -mint vinegar, 172
Light fruit cake, 62
Lime: juice, note on use of, 12; tart, 111; tea bread, 20; tea cakes, 82
Linzer cakes, 84
Liver, chicken; chopped, 183; chopped with mushrooms, 184; pâté en croûte, 200

Mango papaya chutney, 165
Maple syrup: as an ingredient, 13; Vermont whole wheat bread, 23; -walnut sauce, 141
Marjoram vinegar, 171
Marmalade petits fours, 92
Marzipan: chocolate-coated, 134; cocoa-dusted, 133

Mayonnaise, herb and caper, 174
Mediterranean: herb bread, 34; tart, 217
Meringues, mocha, 86
Mincemeat: pear, 161; pear mincemeat tart, 119
Mint: apple mint chutney, 164; chocolate mint wafers, 131; cocoa mint patties, 136; lemon mint tea, 239; lemon mint vinegar, 172; minted pears, 153; pastel mint patties, 135; true mint jelly, 150
Miss Elizabeth Holahan's fine tea wafers, 85
Mocha: -flavored coffee, 238; fudge, 131; meringues, 86
Mock game pâté, 205
Moroccan bread, 36
Mother's Day cake, 49
Mrs. Beeton's almond cake, 53
Mrs. Isabella Beeton's unrivalled plum pudding, 63
Mulled cider mix, 233
Mushroom(s): and chicken livers, chopped, 184; marinated, 185; tart, 219
Mustard shallot butter, 180

Nectarine custard tart, 113
Nut(s): glazed spiced, 134; note on use of, 13; rose pecans, 136; spiced almonds, 190; spiced nuts, 191; sugared pecans, 138; wafers, 87; wafers, Florentine, 88

Oats, steel-cut, note on use of, 13
Oatmeal: apple oatmeal bread, 15
Old-fashioned birthday cake, 54
Old rose potpourri, 236
Onions: tarte a l'oignon, 225
Orange(s): cranberry orange conserve, 160; cranberry orange tea cake, (Christmas tea cake), 18; -chocolate tart, 114; -flavored coffee, 238; orange flower cakes, 88; peel, candied, 126; pomander, 234; -spiced tea, 239; tea cake, 21; walnut sauce, 141; wedding cakes, 89
Orange flower water; note on use of, 13; orange flower cakes, 88
Othello sauce, 175

Packaging, gift, 7
Papaya: mango papaya chutney, 165
Parmesan: note on use of, 12; herb Parmesan biscuits, 194
Parsley pesto, 176
Pastel mint patties, 135

Pastry crusts, 98–101; cheese, 226; flaky pie, 101; pâté, 199; rich tart, 102; savory tarts and pies, 213; sour cream tart, 103
Pâtés: aspic for, 200; chicken liver en croûte, 200; de compagne, 207; duck en croûte, 202; mock game, 205; pastry for, 199; spinach artichoke, 208; summer terrine, 210; to weight, 198
Peach(es): brandied, 152; jam, spiced, 156
Pear(s): -chocolate tart, 116; cranberry pear chutney, 165; -cranberry tart, 118; -ginger jam, 155; -ginger sauce, 156; mincemeat, 161; -mincemeat tart, 119; minted pears, 153; Seckel pear chutney, 168
Pecan(s): chocolate pecan pie, 106; glazed, 134; rose, 136; sugared, 138
Peppers, roasted, 186
Peppercorn butter, green, 180
Pesto, 175
Petits fours, 90
Pies. See Tarts and Pies
Pine forest potpourri, 236
Plum(s): conserve, 162; -walnut cream tart, 119
Plum pudding, Mrs. Isabella Beeton's unrivalled, 63
Pomanders, 234
Potpourris: old rose, 236; pine forest, 236; summer meadow, 236
Preserves: apple mint chutney, 164; apricot conserve, 158; beet conserve, 159; blueberry jam,, 154; brandied peaches, 152; chestnuts in brandy syrup, 151; cranberry orange conserve, 160; cranberry pear chutney, 165; mango papaya chutney, 165; minted pears, 153; pear ginger jam, 155; pear mincemeat, 161; plum conserve, 162; quince chutney, 167; rose petal jelly, 147; sage tracklement, 148; Seckel pear chutney, 168; spiced peach jam, 156; sweet violet jelly, 149; strawberry preserves, 157; true mint jelly, 150
Provençal sauce, 177
Pub loaf, 37
Pumpkin cider bread, 22

Quiches. See Tarts and Pies, savory
Quiche Lorraine, 214
Quick breads. See Breads, quick
Quince chutney, 167

Rich tart crust, 102
Rolled cookies: apricot-filled, 95; chocolate leaves, 96; dough for, 94

Rose hips, note on use of, 13
Rose petals: jelly, 147; pecans, 136; potpourri, 236; tea, 240
Rosewater, note on use of, 13
Rye bread, cottage, 29

Sachets, 235
Sage: tracklement, 148; vinegar, 172
Sauces, dessert: butterscotch, 139; chocolate, 140; hard, 65; maple walnut, 141; orange walnut, 141; pear ginger, 142
Sauces, savory: caper sauce, 173; herb and caper mayonnaise, 174; Othello sauce, 175; parsley pesto, 176; pesto, 175; Provençal cause, 177; tomato chutney, 177
Savories. See individual entries for Butters, Crackers, Nuts, and Spreads
Savory tart crust, 213
Scallops. See Sea quiche
Sea quiche, 220
Seckel pear chutney, 168
Seed cake, 55
Sesame: -Cheddar crackers, 196; oat crackers, 195
Shrimp: artichoke shrimp quiche, 214; butter, 187
Smoked salmon: quiche, 221; spread, 187
Smoked trout spread, 188
Sour cream: -chive bread, 38; tart crust, 103
Spiced almonds, 190
Spiced coffee, 237–8
Spiced fruit cake, 66
Spiced nuts, 191
Spiced peach jam, 156
Spiced tea, 239–40
Spinach: -artichoke pâté, 208; -Roquefort quiche, 222; -tomato pie, 223
Spreads: caper butter, 181; caponata, 182; chopped chicken livers, 183; chopped chicken livers and mushrooms, 184; shrimp butter, 187; smoked salmon spread, 187; smoked trout spread, 188; Stilton butter, 188; tarama spread, 189
Squash. See Summer pie
Stilton cheese: butter, 189; leek Stilton quiche, 216
Strawberry: kiwi strawberry tart, 110; preserves, 157; strawberry almond tart, 121
Sugarplums, 137
Summer meadow potpourri, 236
Summer pie, 224
Summer terrine, 210

Surprise cakes, 92
Sweet potato pie, Kentucky, 109
Sweet violet jelly, 149
Swiss thins, 193

Tarama spread, 189
Tarragon vinegar, 172
Tarte a l'oignon, 225
Tarts and Pies, savory: artichoke shrimp, 214; asparagus, 214; crabmeat, 216; leek Stilton, 216; Mediterranean, 217; mushroom, 219; sea, 220; smoked salmon, 221; spinach Roquefort, 222; spinach tomato, 223; summer, 224; tarte a l'oignon, 225; torta rustica, 226
Tarts and Pies, sweet: apple almond, 104; apricot custard, 114; banana chocolate, 116; chocolate fudge, 105; chocolate pecan, 106; green grape, 107; Kentucky sweet potato, 109; kiwi strawberry, 110; lime, 111; nectarine custard, 113; orange chocolate, 114; pear chocolate, 116; pear cranberry, 118; pear mincemeat, 119; plum-walnut cream, 119; strawberry almond, 121
Teas: lemon mint, 239; orange spice, 239; rose, 240; spiced, 240
Tea cakes and breads. See Breads, quick
Terrines. See Pâtés
Tomato chutney, 177
Tony's birthday cake, 56

Torta rustica, 226
Tortes. See Cakes
True mint jelly, 150
Truffles, chocolate, 132
Twelfth cake, 58

Valentine, chocolate cake, 47
Vermont whole wheat bread, 23
Violet jelly, sweet, 149
Vinegars, flavored: basil, 171; dill, 171; herbed red wine, 170; herbed white wine, 171; lemon mint, 172; marjoram, 171; sage, 172; tarragon, 172

Wafers: chocolate mint, 131; Florentine nut, 88; Miss Elizabeth Holahan's fine tea, 85; nut, 87
Walnut(s): maple walnut sauce, 141; orange walnut sauce, 141; pie crust, 105; plum-walnut cream tart, 119; torte. See Tony's birthday cake
Wedding cakes, small: chocolate, 75; orange, 89
Wheat bread: country wheat bread, 30; Vermont whole wheat bread, 23
White Christmas cake, 68

Yeast, proofing, 25
Yeast breads. See Breads, yeast

Zucchini bread, 24

Helen Hecht and Linda LaBate Mushlin are neighbors in Rochester, New York. The idea for this book evolved when they both found themselves spending immoderate amounts of time in their kitchens and regularly sharing many of their culinary innovations.